AF473404

THE PERFECT STOCK:

How a 7000% move was set-up, started and finished in an astonishing 52 weeks

By

Brad Koteshwar

1663 Liberty Drive, Suite 200
Bloomington, Indiana 47403
(800) 839-8640
www.AuthorHouse.com

This book is a work of fiction. Places, events, and situations in this story are purely fictional and any resemblance to actual persons, living or dead, is coincidental.

First published by AuthorHouse 09/27/04

ISBN: 1-4184-8688-4 (sc)

Printed in the United States of America
Bloomington, Indiana

This book is printed on acid-free paper.

TABLE OF CONTENTS

CHAPTER 1:
APRIL 13, 2004, TUESDAY MORNING - THE JOB 1

CHAPTER 2:
APRIL 13, 2004, TUESDAY AFTERNOON - IDENTIFYING THE INSIDERS 9

CHAPTER 3:
APRIL 13, 2004, TUESDAY EVENING - THE SPECULATOR 14

CHAPTER 4:
APRIL 14, 2004, WEDNESDAY MORNING - THE LARGEST SHAREHOLDER 29

CHAPTER 5:
APRIL 14, 2004, WEDNESDAY AFTERNOON - THE MONEY MEN 33

CHAPTER 6:
APRIL 14, 2004, WEDNESDAY EVENING - THE SPECULATOR'S BASICS 39

CHAPTER 7:
APRIL 15, 2004, THURSDAY MORNING - THE STOCKBROKER 48

CHAPTER 8:
APRIL 15, 2004, THURSDAY AFTERNOON - THE POOL OPERATOR 61

CHAPTER 9:
THE SPECULATOR'S BASICS - CONTINUED 67

CHAPTER 10:
APRIL 16, 2004, FRIDAY MORNING - THE SHAREHOLDER, AGAIN 74

CHAPTER 11:
APRIL 16, 2004, FRIDAY AFTERNOON - THE SPECULATOR'S OPERATION 78

CHAPTER 12:
THE CLASSIC POOL OPERATOR 91

CHAPTER 13:
APRIL 17, 2004, SATURDAY - THE REPORT TAKES SHAPE 107

CHAPTER 14:
APRIL 19, 2004, MONDAY - THE END IS NEAR 110

CHAPTER 15:
SOME OF THE OUTSIDERS 117

CHAPTER 16:
THE SHORT SQUEEZE GETS SHORTY 123

CHAPTER 17:
THE WEEK THAT WAS 131

CHAPTER 18:
MORE OUTSIDERS 134

CHAPTER 19:
COVER YOUR SHORTS.................................. 151

CHAPTER 20:
WAR STORIES.. 156

CHAPTER 21:
NO FREE LUNCH 172

CHAPTER 22:
SOME IDLE THOUGHTS.................................. 179

CHAPTER 23:
THE AFTERMATH 182

To my wife, who like the market, is always right

AUTHOR'S NOTES:

This is a work of fiction. The trades offered and the identities of the characters in this story are purely fictional and creations of the writer's imagination. Any reflections of the characters or their actions to any person living or dead is by pure coincidence and without any intention. The dates do correspond to the actual movement of the stock price of Taser International - ticker symbol TASR. However, to simplify the understanding of the stock market to the lay person, no stock splits have been accounted for. Both prices and the volume of shares traded are discussed assuming no splits have occurred.

PROLOGUE

Memorial day weekend had come and gone. It was early June 2001. For the insiders at Taser it was turning out to be one of the slowest IPOs in years. An IPO or the Initial Public Offering is the first day of trade when a stock first comes into the open market. A private company owned and run by private individuals becomes a public company when it sells its shares to the general public. And thus the public is now able to be part of the ownership of the company through purchase of the company's stock and then becomes a shareholder of the company. The hey-day of the internet bubble was gone. Gone were the days when IPOs would come to the market and within days their price would be two or three times their IPO price.

Taser started its IPO day quietly. So quietly that besides the insiders hardly anybody traded the stock that day. The opening price was $7/share. It closed at the end of the trading session at $6.85/share. It had traded a mere 16,700 shares that day. The grand total amount that was spent by all trades that took place on Taser stock on its IPO day was a meager $116,000.

The trade was not noticed by anybody other than the handful of insiders.

About 21 months later on April 18, 2003, it was still trading in unnoticeable amounts. In fact, on April 18, 2003, it closed at $5.45/share and traded a total of 66,200 shares. The dollar amount traded on that day was about $360,790. Yet again, the trade was under most folks' radar. Nobody knew it that day. But there would come a day very soon that would show an incredible amount of trade on this stock.

On April 19, 2004, exactly 52 weeks later, Taser would trade over $3 billion…that is billion with a "B" worth of stock. It would hit an intraday high price on that day of $385/share and trade 10 million shares. Almost every stock trader in the country would have heard of it by then. And probably most of the actively trading public would have traded that stock at least once by then. A few would have profited on the stock but many many more would be left holding the bag. Those who profited would be an extremely small minority. The public at large would hardly make a dime on their investment and the vast majority would be left holding papers worth a fraction of what they paid for the stock.

From the April 18, 2003, price of $5.45/share to its high exactly 52 weeks later of $385/share, Taser would have made an incredible 7065% move. A small $5,000 account invested in Taser would be worth over $380,000 within just one year. For the insiders at Taser this would be absolutely the perfect stock. But for the outsiders it would be a far different story.

My involvement with Taser was for less than six weeks. But it would be one of the most rewarding six weeks in my life as a stock trader. The trading lessons I learned during those six weeks would turn out to be priceless in terms of my success over the rest of my life as a stock trader. It would be some time later that I would understand the true value of the lessons I learned then. I knew that we live in a country where ordinary folks can do extraordinary things. Which is what made America so great. I was going to realize once again that ordinary looking stocks can make extraordinary moves. That is what made the American stock market so great.

CHAPTER 1:

APRIL 13, 2004, TUESDAY MORNING - THE JOB

It was early spring of 2004. It was a time like no other. Martha Stewart, the domestic diva, had just been convicted of lying to the feds. Dennis Kozlowski, the poster child for the spoiled rotten rich American CEOs was on trial in New York. Dennis had been a bad boy. He had apparently stolen millions from Tyco, his own company. Dick Grasso, the chairman of the New York Stock Exchange, had been ousted from his position over a furor about an exorbitant pay package. Grasso's pay had been almost $200 million, which he had helped push through for himself. Ken Lay and his boys, who ran Enron, had duped thousands of shareholders to the tune of millions of dollars. Some of the good old boys were being naughty again. But the rules that applied to them and other corporate insiders would be far different from the ones that applied to the rest of us common folks.

The devastating three-year bear market was behind us. Most portfolios had been ravaged. The one that lost the least was the best performing account. As they say, in the land of the blind, the one-eyed man is king. And now the stock market had bounced back significantly from the bear market lows of October 2002. In fact, in 18 months, the Nasdaq had bounced 90%. It was as if the public had forgotten the carnage left behind by the three-year bear market. Gambling in stocks was in vogue again. Stock market tips were available a dime a dozen and stock trading was rampant once again. It was time again for the game to come to an end. The fun had lasted a little bit too long. Once again the party had to end.

I was an old hand at trading. I had started out trading in commodities almost 20 years ago and had switched to stocks over the past 15 years. It was not the normal route. Most folks start with stocks and end up in commodities and not the other way around. I had found I could make similar returns in stocks as one could in commodities without having to take the larger risks and I could now avoid the sleepless nights that haunt a commodities trader.

I was always scared whenever I took a position in the market. That came from commodities trading. And this actually had saved me many times in the stock market from taking insurmountable losses. I could not take losses. If the price went 10% against my position, I would start to get nervous. This was a mechanism I had developed that was a result of many experiences of losses trading commodities. In my early days I did not have it in me to sell for a loss. How could anybody sell to take a loss? It just did not make sense back in my early days. Now, after many years of experience, I cannot take a position without allocating a fixed amount as the maximum risk that I can take on any trade I place. In the beginning I found it hard to execute the sell for loss as risk-protection. But after many large losses I started relying on stop-orders. This way the orders would be in place as soon as I entered a position. Thus, I protected my account from myself. I would avoid being placed in a position where I could talk myself out of a good decision.

I had learned about market cycles over the years. I knew more than most folks. And I knew enough to know that I did not know it all. That itself was knowing something. I also learned that nobody out there knows it all. The folks who act like they know it all are more likely to be wrong than right. The lessons from the markets were absolute to me. Cash is king. Without cash I could not make any commitments in the market. Even if the best opportunity is presented on a silver platter, it would be of no use to me if I did not have cash to put into positions. I would learn to remain in long periods of cash until I found a stock that was in a clearly visible trend.

I am an early riser. I was up and was on my second cup of black coffee. I worked from home and I had a nice little office inside my home in Scottsdale, Arizona. I had the business sections of the Arizona Republic and New York Times spread open on my desk. It was my routine. I was glancing at the headlines on the first page of the business sections on both the papers. Both the papers were laid out side by side. The phone rang. As I picked up the phone I saw the headlines were almost identical in both the papers. They both read something akin to "Taser soars yet again in anticipation of stellar earnings."

"Hello." I said into the phone.

"Hello, stranger." It was Joe. Joe and I had started out together as commodities brokers in the 1980s. He had gone on to do very well as a venture capitalist. His consortium was made mainly of some heavy hitting clients he had developed during his commodities days. His timing had been perfect as he and his clients cashed in big-time on the 1990s boom of technology companies. He and his people had helped launch many ventures which eventually went on to become successful IPOs on the stock market. He was now a serious player on a serious level. I had maintained my own stock trading and market research operation. Since I was a lone operator, my independence was appreciated some times in the market circles. When I heard his voice, I knew he was calling because he wanted my investigative and interpretative skills. Joe knew I had a way of interpreting the information I dug up that was on par with some of the best in the business.

"Joe! How are you? It has been months. Hope all is well?"

"It is all good," he came directly to the point. He was always direct. Nowadays he was busier than ever and never wasted time on small talk unless he was on the golf course. "I want you to look into the Taser story."

"What would you like to know besides the story everywhere of its soaring stock price?" I asked.

"Everything."

"Everything everything?"

"Well….everything to do with who is trading, how are they trading and what kind of trading is going on with the stock. Use your trading skills and also your research skills to see what kinds of folks are involved. And what are they doing with their holdings," Joe replied. He continued, "I am wiring the usual fee today to your account. I will wire an additional exact same amount to you next Tuesday. In effect, I have doubled your fee because I need the findings by Monday morning before the market opens."

I stood up slowly. I took a slow deep breath. He had just doubled my going rate for less than six days of work. It was work I needed. I was going to take it. But something in Joe's voice said that he wanted me badly. I was going to see just how badly he needed me.

"Joe, that is a lot of work and the time constraint is tight. I'll need complete access to your research staff." As a venture capitalist, he had a very effective investigative research staff. But they were all computer intensive people. I figured he wanted field work. There was no other reason for him to call me but for my field work. I continued sensing his urgency, "And I will need a $100,000 bonus to drop all that I am currently working on. I have to renegotiate my current commitments which will make some of my clients very unhappy. I need compensation for the potential lost jobs that will be taken elsewhere due to my failure to meet deadlines already committed to." I knew enough about stocks to see that when Joe wants a full picture of a stock that goes from $5 to over $300 in 12 months, then something big was brewing. He did not have to know that the things I was working on currently did not have any urgency to them. They were all small, boring and quite inane projects from clients who were novices in the markets.

"Done. I need the findings by email before Monday's market open. Otherwise, the deal is off," Joe stated and he hung up.

I sat down. I pulled my yellow legal pad out. I wrote down the following numbers:

$75,000 advance

$75,000 at completion

$100,000 bonus

Total $250,000 in six days

This was going to be my best week ever. Little did I know what lay in store over the next five weeks.

The first call I made was to Joe's research staff. VJ answered the phone. He was very good at his job.

Information is everywhere nowadays since we live in an information age. And there is an overload of data as more is available if one seeks to get more information. But what separates me from most is that I know where to look for the right information. And I had learned the importance of discarding the unimportant data. Then to interpret the right data correctly was the final key. It came easily to me due to much practice and years of experience. I told VJ to expect a short email from me within the hour listing the information I was seeking. And I told him that I needed the information I asked to be sent back to me before lunch.

After about an hour I made my second call. It was to my bank. Joe's $75,000 was already in my account. Joe always meant business.

I put together my email to VJ. I asked him to give me complete background and details he had about the following players:

1. Identity and background data on the biggest single stock holder of Taser

2. The underwriting investment banker who handled Taser's IPO and brought the stock to the market

3. The best connected stock broker in the valley that has close ties to Taser's IPO investment banker

4. Which commission house and/or research service started touting Taser stock over the most recent 2-3 weeks

And I also requested a complete set of daily and weekly charts for Taser. The charts, I asked him to fax to me.

I went to lunch.

CHAPTER 2:

APRIL 13, 2004, TUESDAY AFTERNOON - IDENTIFYING THE INSIDERS

After lunch I checked my email. VJ had done his job. He was as good as I had known him to be. I printed the email out. It listed the names and some basic background data as I had requested. I went on to add some additional hand written notes to the printout. I also had the charts I had requested in my fax machine. I read VJ's email printout with my notes on them.

It read:

David Richey: One of the owners and founders of Taser. Taser was his brainchild and was founded by him a few years ago and the company specialized in making stun guns. The stun guns sold under the Taser brand. He was smart, ambitious and well connected with the law enforcement community. After all, he started his business off by selling his products first to the police departments of the major U.S. cities. The product was highly successful and met many of the law enforcement officers' basic requirements of subduing a suspect without causing serious damage to the suspect. Thus, many lawsuits were avoided by the law enforcement departments around the country. David had contemplated taking his company public during the go-go days of the late 1990s. But by the time he could put his ducks in a row, the bear market was already in full swing. His investment banker - Sachs and Sachs - advised him wisely that money was leaving the stock market and it was not a good time to go public. Then in the spring of 2001 he had started laying the ground work to take his company public. By the time Sachs and Sachs was ready to go with the Initial Public Offering (IPO), David had learned from his contacts at the CIA and the FBI that there was some serious danger of terrorism. Islamic fundamentalists had been escalating their terror on westerners and western interests for a decade by then. As the summer of 2001 came near, David's CIA friends were anticipating something big. David Richey had learned from his sources that this time it was going to be within the United States. As a result he had pushed Sachs and Sachs to place the IPO on the market at the earliest. As it turned, the stock went public less than 12 weeks before the 9/11 attacks. He was the largest single shareholder of Taser stocks.

Sachs & Sachs: An investment banker who underwrote the Taser IPO. An IPO is handled by an investment banker with solid connections within the venture capital and the investment capital worlds. The main responsibility of a good investment banker is to bring to the market a heretofore unheard stock and create enough buzz and hype to excite the market and the buyers to part with their cash in exchange for stock of the new public company. Then once this first little excitement and buzz is created and the stock becomes listed, the true responsibility of making sure that the stock becomes liquid and well distributed over the course of many years comes in. This takes large amounts of capital as the investment banker has to arrange enough buying at market lows and/or market reactions. And at the same time, create enough selling so as to not let the stock move so fast that the interest dies seemingly as buyers may believe the stock is too highly priced. And at the same time a very fast moving stock may invite heavy short sellers who short the stock and may drive the price of the stock to be too volatile. A very volatile stock then becomes much harder to distribute as many folks shy away from volatile issues.

John Romano: The lead stock broker who worked with Sachs and Sachs on the Taser IPO. An investment banker who wants to push and create a buzz about a new stock coming to market relies on a handful of closely selected efficient brokerages with a large base of big money clients. The IPO is first offered to the big money buyers. The lead brokers do the sales job and lead the charge in hyping an IPO. This arouses immediate buzz and excitement for the new issue. The race started well is more likely to end well.

Romano was from the North East and still maintained his clients and contact base there even though now he called Scottsdale his home.

Santos and Holland: The commission house and research analyst who had started touting Taser stock over the recent most 2-3 weeks. Alex Santos was a well-known analyst and also a newsletter writer. His newsletters were well subscribed to by many leading brokerage and commission houses. The subscriptions to his writings were quite pricey. I made a hand written note that I had very little knowledge of this entity.

I added a fifth name to the list - Boyd Hunt. Hardly anybody knew Boyd. He was not an insider. As a matter of fact, Boyd was really a classic outsider. But his trades would place him in a spot that was as good as an insider's spot.

Boyd was a friend and was among the most discreet and unassuming men I had ever met. I had known him for years. I had met him years ago when I was a commodities broker. And I had found him to be very easy to talk to. He was always generous with his time with me. He was also a very successful stock trader. He was a true professional. They did not make many of his kinds of traders nowadays. My first call that afternoon was to Boyd Hunt. I needed a quick brush up of the stock market psychology and basics offered to me like only he could offer. Boyd had the ability to simplify the most complex of matters. Not that I needed the lessons but I wanted to produce a full report for Joe. It did not matter whether Joe would pay any attention to all of it or not, I was going to give him more than his money's worth. After all, he had just committed to a $250,000 investment in my report.

CHAPTER 3:

APRIL 13, 2004, TUESDAY EVENING - THE SPECULATOR

I drove to Boyd's modern, spacious and expensive home perched on the hill. He had agreed to see me and discuss matters relating to the stock market and specifically about Taser over drinks. The view was gorgeous. The desert sun was setting which cast a beautiful striking pink sky as the backdrop over the pool. The pool had a zero edge. One of those pools that looks like it has a sudden drop off over the hill into the valley below. It was an illusion but the effect off the hill was stunning.

Boyd offered me black coffee and Hennessy X.O. We parked ourselves poolside. He began, "Why the sudden interest now in stocks? The market seems to be topping around here at least for the intermediate term. You should be looking to go fishing now. Not to buy stocks. And more importantly your interest in Taser is surprising since I am now looking to get out of Taser shortly."

"I am doing some background work on Taser for a large client. It is now headline news. There is talk about stellar earnings report coming out next Tuesday. I thought I could pick your brains about the stock," I offered. "Obviously Boyd, everything about you will be kept out of the report. You know that." I confirmed to him what he knew about me. I never betrayed confidences. And Boyd, who was a stickler for anonymity, appreciated this more than most.

"You have to be careful when dealing with the markets. I suppose there is no need to tell you that since you are an old trader like myself. I am always wary and respectful of the market. I have been bitten severely many times by the market. And the bite has been deadly every time I had become arrogant. I am now always humble when dealing with the market. So if I sound defensive and somewhat skeptical of the majority of what goes on in the market, it is due to my plain humility. Now that you have my disclaimer that will explain my serious skepticism about the stock market, where would you like to start?" Boyd said as he took a sip of his cognac.

It is not everybody who gets to listen to one of the true masters of the stock market. Boyd was from an earlier generation and the wisdom was always understated. And he always offered the complete truth. He made it plain that the dangers in the markets far outweighed its ability to be generous. He was unknown to most of the in crowd on Wall Street. As is normally the case, the more well known somebody is on the Street more the chances are that such a person's best days are long gone. It is similar to being a blue chip stock. Its best days of great growth and movements are long gone. Having finished its great move up through its great growth years, it reaches a mature phase where the rate of growth is slow and steady. Once someone becomes well known in the financial circles, his ego starts to work against him as he becomes, in his own mind, more important than he really is. And that is the first step toward mediocrity. Ego and self-importance have no place in the markets.

Boyd Hunt was the only one of his kind I knew. He avoided attention, stayed away from the limelight and he went about his operation in complete silence and detachment from the rest of the world. There was no agenda and no self-promotion on Boyd's part. I had to take full advantage of the opportunity. I took my pad out and said, "Boyd, if you could, please start with the basics of stock market speculation tonight. After I have done some digging, I'll have to come back to you for a detailed trading lesson and your trade executions on Taser. I hope to be back within the next couple of days, if that is acceptable?"

What Boyd knows about the market is priceless. If used correctly over time, the knowledge he can impart can make anybody wealthy. I was judicious in my note taking that evening.

Later that night I sat down on my computer at home and began typing all that I had heard from Boyd that evening. I was typing till late into the night. I printed out the write-up. I picked up the stack of the typed papers and went to sit in my favorite chair in front of the TV. I hit the mute button on the remote to kill the volume on the TV. CNBC TV was on. And some pundit was hyping the stock market. The European markets were already open. This pundit was claiming that a global expansion was on its way. The mute on my remote put a stop to his hype. And I began to read what Boyd had to say that evening. It was in Boyd's own words. That was the only way to write it and it went like this:

Nothing in the stock market happens without reason. And the folks with the money make things happen. And there is reason behind every move. The reason may or may not be obvious and in many cases it never becomes clear. Most of the times it does not become clear to even the most astute of observers. Should the astute observer figure out the reason behind any specific move, it is most times clear only in hindsight.

All participants in the market are human beings. There are no aliens or animal participants. It follows, therefore, everything that happens in the market is due to human action. Humans are the only buyers and sellers. The price settles at the end of the day at a level where all the buyers and the sellers for a particular stock come to a balanced agreement for a price for that day. What happens intraday is mainly noise.

I have learned that to watch the tape (computer screen) during the market hours is like a slow death. Every price tick up and down just drives me nuts. And I end up making on the spot stupid decisions. Then I see some news flash on my trading window and suddenly I am swayed one way or another on that stock. So I go ahead and place some order on the spot thinking of how I can make money off the latest newsflash. Even though I know very well that the news only confirms the move. The move always occurs well before the news. The smart money usually sells into good news only to buy it back at a reaction. That is because the smart money had discounted the news weeks before it became news. When the news is released and the public gets excited, the smart money can sell into the increased volume of buying from the public.

When I watch the tape, it turns out to be nothing more than an online casino. And in a casino, online or not, the odds are against me. I cannot be a successful speculator if I do not pay attention to odds of wins. The only time I have made big money in the stock market is when I have relied on myself and nobody else. And it has always been a successful venture when I made a small first commitment and added larger pyramid positions to my first commitment. And all of my most successful trades involved never watching the tape but relying on stop-orders.

I find that my interpretation and decisions based on my own interpretations work well for me. And they work best with distance from the noise and the news of the moment. The distance allows me to see the market from my own eyes instead of relying on someone else's view.

If I want to buy a car, I would go to the dealership, test drive the car that looks and feels right to me. Then if the price is right, I make the decision to buy. This way I have seen the car with my own eyes. I have felt it in my own hands. I have test-driven the car myself. I would never buy a car because some car broker calls me on the phone and describes the car to me and makes a sales pitch of how great the car is.

If you were looking to buy a house, would you not go and look at the house? Perhaps more than a couple of visits are made to the house. The neighborhood is checked out. Is it crime ridden? Is it in the right school district? Are there any hospitals, grocery stores, shopping centers, entertainment centers, restaurants, etc. near by? It is inspected by an independent inspector. All appliances are checked to make sure everything is in working order. An appraisal is done. Only then would one consider buying the house. You would never buy a house based on the broker 's description of the house on the phone.

But humans will buy large amounts of stock based on a phone call from a broker. Why is that we make such decisions? There is only one answer. It is the promise of riches. The only reason one buys stock is to make gains. In most cases, the buy is made to enrich ourselves rather quickly. It is no different in that respect from a casino. We bet in a casino to enrich ourselves, quickly.

The public has no idea of probabilities. They only believe in the possibilities. It is possible one could become an instant multimillionaire at a casino. It has been known to happen once in a while. It is possible that one can land a true winner in the stock market and make millions. It has been known to happen sometimes. It is possible that folks can win multimillion dollar lottery jackpots. It has happened a few times before. But just because something has happened before does not mean that it is probable. It certainly is possible. But how many of us sit down to think about the probabilities? The only consistent winner in the stock market is the one who places his commitments based on probabilities and not on possibilities.

There is a thin line between a gambler and a speculator. The gambler is everywhere. We are a nation of gamblers. There are casinos everywhere now. Betting on sporting events is a way of life among the young, old, fanatics and the machismo. Horse racing is prevalent everywhere. With the advent of the internet, there is gambling everywhere on all things. Including stocks. There are slot machines at the airport in Las Vegas. So one can lose money while wasting time waiting for their flights. Next thing you know, some genius will install slots on the airplanes so one can gamble away while flying.

Successful speculation, unlike gambling, is hardly common. In fact, a successful speculator is a rare breed. Though when the public places blame on any violent move in the market on the shoulders of speculators, it would seem that successful speculators abound. Speculation is placing commitments only when odds are in one's favor. The action is not taken by a speculator unless and until the odds favor him. The gambler will make commitments without regard to the odds of wins.

The shakedown in the stock market is in the promise of fortune. This is what brings money into the market. There is a 'deal of the day' for any buyer at all times. The market could be in the depths of a severe bear market but if you ask a broker, "what looks good?" he will always find a way to spend your money. There is always a stock that is "ready to make a move."

America is a capitalist society. It means more the capital, more the society. It is all interconnected. The stock market is a vehicle to raise capital for a company to invest and grow. In most cases, it enriches the owners of the company (shareholders) when a stock goes public via an IPO. There is instant wealth created. But wealth does not grow out of trees. There is big money that is used to buy to set up the gig. The set-up takes a long time. Many times it lasts years and years and may even last decades. The move itself takes a far less time than the set-up. It requires a lot of patience to be the big money players.

There is only one way to get the public excited in buying a stock. That is by showing rising prices. One only looks to buy a stock whose price is rising. Nobody wants to buy a stock whose price is falling. There is only one way to prove that a stock's price is rising. The stock does that by plotting a series of higher price highs and higher price lows. If a stock makes new higher price high than a prior price high and then at price reactions makes a higher price low than a prior low, it shows the tendency to rise. There is no better way to market a stock than setting it on a course of such an uptrend. Suddenly there is interest within the public to buy such a "winner."

The investment bank or the underwriter which helps issue the IPO helps set the ball in motion. In an incentive based system the investment bank (the underwriter) is given a percentage of shares outstanding as a fee to help distribute the stock to the public. Distribution of stock means that the stock ends up in as wide a universe of holders as possible. Which means a large number of holders will end up holding a smaller and smaller percentage of the stock's outstanding shares. This way no one set of buyers can move the stock by themselves. The investment banker (underwriter) has to arrange through its own friendly deep-pocket agents to buy and support the stock at reactions. This will stop the stock from a total sell off. Every time the stock falls in price, it is considered to be a reaction to its prior move up. At such price pullbacks, the stock is bought by the underwriter and his agents to support its price. Thus for example, if the stock moves up 10 points - it is allowed to react five points.

The reaction is always ensured to be less than the move up. And each reaction is supported at higher and higher prices. The stage is set, completed and the game fully played out. At the end of the play, the public has poured large amounts of funds into the stock from its inception as an IPO to the time that the stock is fully distributed. And along the way some riches are made by the select few. It is worse than the lottery. In a lottery the public contributes to the pot and at least the lottery winner is chosen randomly. In the stock market there is nothing random. The public contributes to the pot, but the winners are not randomly chosen. Like it was said before, in the stock market everything happens for a reason.

You know for years I used to write a newsletter. I would make stock picks and more importantly I would make comments on the stock market's general trend. I would try and make the point that the best odds of wins are when one limits one's trades to only periods of confirmed trends in the market. More importantly, it would always payoff to be buying only during market up trends and to be staying in cash during downtrends or uncertain trends.

The need to limit one's trades was constantly mentioned in the newsletter. I would try and direct my subscribers to trade no more than 5-10 trades in any given year. I myself would lean toward five trades a year. But you know the way the human mind works. It does not like to sit still. The idle mind is the devil's workshop. Sitting still meant doing nothing. There would be periods where one would have no buys. And in other periods one would sit with their holdings. But it always involved sitting still. The actual action of buying and selling itself had to be rare.

And I tried to convey to my readers that more the number of trades more the losses. That is the way the probabilities are stacked up in the stock market. For example, if there was a 30% probability of wins, one would take seven losses in 10 trades. If one traded 20 times, the number of losses would increase to 14 out of 20 trades. And worse still, the losses would come first and by the time gains started to show, the losses would have eaten up most of the trading capital. But we humans do not like to hear such realities. The promise of riches had to be kept alive and well. Especially, when there are whole bunches of pundits on TV and on the internet and in print media who are all always hyping some stock or the other. Humans like to find views from so-called pundits that would coincide with their own internal bias. Think about it. If I wanted to be long the market I would be inclined to listen to and believe the bulls. If I wanted to short the market, I would be inclined to pay attention to the bears.

Constant bullishness would win more subscribers than the constantly correct market calls. I was in cash during most of the three-year bear market of 2000-2002. And I offered the same interpretation and reasoning to my readers. The odds of making any decent gains in long positions were not in the favor of the trader. And under such market conditions it would be best to stay in cash. There was no need to buy anything. In fact, my suggestion was clear and "do not buy stocks" was my mantra. Of course, hardly anybody wanted to listen to such messages. It is all right if one hears the 'do not buy' message for some weeks. But hardly anybody wishes to hear such a constant drum beat for months on end. That is depressing. Even though it was the right move.

The problem is that since most advisors cannot time the market, they assume that it cannot be done. Let me tell you something. While I cannot catch the bottom and the top of a move, I can definitely time the periods of increased odds of winning in the market. I would only suggest trading in such time periods of increased odds. But the public cannot wait. They find that money burns holes in their pockets. And spending cash to make more cash is touted with the line that, "you have to put your cash to use." If my cash is not taking losses, I consider that putting the cash to use.

In the end, after some years I closed up my newsletter. I find that it is best to just make my trades my way and head in or out of the market based on my own read of the situation. The gains I make confirm that I am right. If I am wrong, I get stopped out with a minor loss. You trade in silence. If one advertises or claims wins, people do not believe you or worse still they are jealous of you. If one shows losses, people are quick to put you down. What most folks do not know is that over 85% of people who trade in the stock market underperform the market. That includes all the professionals and novices alike. Therefore, the joke about throwing darts at a stock table can make better returns than the market averages. And there is more than some truth to it.

We live in a society that seeks instant gratification. All of us want immediate action and results. None of us has the old-fashioned patience anymore. None of us wants to wait for anything. It is even more prevalent in the stock market. We want to make triple digit returns in days and weeks when in reality it takes weeks and months. We see that in shot gun weddings and divorces our young people go through nowadays. Nobody wants to work at things anymore. If something does not work on the first or second attempts, most folks will throw in the towel. And folks start looking elsewhere for a faster and quicker satisfaction.

Most of us will try our hand at one method of trading and if a failure shows up once or twice, we will quit. And we start looking at some other method of stock trading. Folks will be on a constant quest for the magic answer. The answer is right in front of us. It takes many years of experience and learning and the ability to "sticking to it" before any reasonable success can be expected in the stock market. Just how many will work at learning and studying the market? How many will take the time and effort and show extreme patience that is needed?

From my experience as a newsletter publisher of some years, I can tell you that very few can achieve success in the market. This is because very few will exercise the patience and the discipline that is needed. Everybody cuts corners, skips rules, makes exceptions to the rules of trading, rationalizes, loses patience, and will move onto some newer, quicker way to beat the market as touted by some new schemer who sells to the public his "new way to beat the market." Whether it is computer generated models, software, options or futures. They all are just another way to lose money. I always remind myself that if I cannot make money in stocks, how can I make money in options or futures? Options and futures are more risky and more leveraged so logic would dictate that I would lose more there than in straight stock trading.

And one other rule I have is that I cannot make money on a $1 million account if I cannot make money of a $100,000 account. The amount of trading capital does not dictate the rate of returns. If I make mistakes on a $100,000 account, I will make the same mistakes on a $1 million account.

There is only one way to beat the market. That is to learn the lessons of the market oneself and try to recognize the lessons offered by masters of yester years. The old masters who have long gone do, through their writings and experiences, confirm the lessons we ourselves will learn in the markets. Those who claim to be successful in today's markets but will never caution us against the pitfalls are more likely than not doing injustice to their readers.

But in this game of cat and mouse, no one group can be faulted. The experienced trader will ask from his readers that some many months of commitment be made to the newsletter before an intelligent judgment can be made about the service. But the reader has no use for many months of commitment - he wants immediate results because there are hundreds of services out there that promise instant results. Therefore, the really good services will not last because they will ask for longer term commitments from their readers. The reader is unwilling to offer such longer term commitments to the newsletter.

Therefore, the newsletter folds or changes its tune to be constantly bullish to appeal to the eternal hopes of the vast majority of the investor public at large. Everybody wants to hear that things are going to get better. And they would rather pay to hear such constant but wrong bullishness rather than be right in the market. Since making the right calls in the market entails being bearish more often than not, it is not appealing to the "hope filled" readership. Hope is eternal. As long as that continues to be the case, the markets will provide ample opportunity for the select few to make fortunes and the vast majority of the public is offered opportunities to spend their money.

I had to fold my newsletter because I was not interested in becoming another run of the mill newsletter that is constantly bullish. Or offer up a large basket of stocks as buys knowing that with a large basket there would be at least some winners. I would not be truthful that way.

I make my bread and butter trading the markets anyway. And I prefer my quiet anonymous way of operating in the market. This way I do not make any enemies and I do not raise anybody's ire. I stay out of the way of the big boys and I do not ruffle any feathers. I do not talk about my trades and I do not talk about the market anymore to anybody. When that rare someone I run into recalls my connection to the market, I excuse myself quickly and generally I will only comment whether the market is tradable or not tradable. Beyond that I stay non-committal and uninvolved in any market conversation.

Thus, ended Boyd's commentary for that night.

CHAPTER 4:

APRIL 14, 2004, WEDNESDAY MORNING - THE LARGEST SHAREHOLDER

David Richey was quite eager to see me when I told him on the phone that I was doing a story on Taser for an independently large investment group. He did not ask me the identity of the investment group that I told him I was representing. He had been a busy man lately. His company was making headlines. The headlines were being made not only due to the incredible stock price advance, but also due to consistently solid earnings growth over the recent most four quarters in a row. Earnings growth had been a phenomenal 100% or higher for each of the past four quarters. He was not shy. He basked in the publicity. Taser was his baby. It had become very successful and he had every reason to be proud. I could not help remembering my reading from last night. Boyd was right. Advancing share prices is the best form of marketing.

I asked him, "You must be very happy now that you are a millionaire 150 times over?" He had held onto his 500,000 shares in Taser from its IPO. At today's price of over $300/share, he was worth every cent of the $150 million on paper. He deflected the question. By now he had become an expert at handling questions.

"The stock price is nothing but a reflection of our tremendous growth and the further excellent prospects of spectacular growth. We have not even touched the overseas markets for our Taser guns, leave alone most of the United States," he responded.

Since I needed to speak with him at least once more in the coming day or two, I decided to soft-ball a hard question. "Your timing of bringing the stock to market with an IPO was impeccable. Would you consider that it was blind luck or did Sachs and Sachs help you make that decision? After all, an IPO just 12-14 weeks before 9/11 could not have been better timed." Sachs and Sachs was the investment banker who had handled Taser's IPO.

"Well, I was thinking of going public as far back as mid-2000. It was Sachs who convinced me to wait as they had forecasted the impending bear market then. I had started working on the IPO once again in early 2001. By the time we came to the market, it just was the process of the IPO that took it until the summer of 2001. The IPO preceding 9/11 was just by happenstance," he replied. He never once alluded to his inside sources at the CIA and the FBI.

So I did it for him. "I was told you have great connections and friends at the Bureau and the Agency besides your vast network of clients in the police departments around the country. Did any of your friends ever indicate to you that during the summer of 2001 they were getting signals of a big terror event within the United States?"

He did not blink and said, "Absolutely not. I did not discuss my business plans and finances with anyone regarding taking the company public. Friends or not."

I had to let it go at that. He would not offer anything along that line of questions. So I reverted to the stock price story. I knew on this topic his pride would let him expound more on my questions. "So, how far of an upside do you still see for Taser's share prices? Can you sustain such tremendous price growth?"

Richey laughed, "With new orders back log and the whole of Europe just being tapped into, I can see a $1000 stock price in the not so distant future." He was now bordering on the ebullient.

"Are you concerned that your bright predictions and forecast may make some folks think you are just talking up your stock since you are a large shareholder?"

"Absolutely not. Just look at our quarterly rate of earnings growth. Sales are increasing at similar rates. For several quarters we have shown triple digit rates of sales and earnings growth. Stock price follows earnings. And earnings are just now accelerating. We see many quarters of huge growth ahead." Richey stood up as an indication that my time was up.

"If you do not mind, I would like to request you give me a few minutes on the phone before the end of the week. I will call you by Friday. If you can take the call, I'll greatly appreciate it as will my clients. I'll promise to keep it short," I said standing up.

"No problem at all," he left the office giving me a firm handshake.

I left his corporate office marveling at the opulence and the rich smell of success there. David did not believe in any cost cutting. He was going to learn the same lessons as many technology darlings of the late 1990s had. He had no need to think about cost cutting, yet. His company was on a tear and things looked fabulous, right now. The future was yet to come.

CHAPTER 5:

APRIL 14, 2004, WEDNESDAY AFTERNOON - THE MONEY MEN

Sachs and Sachs are the money men. You can call them an investment banker, an underwriter or whatever - but the fact is they are the money men. They have money of their own, they have connections and clients who have money and they have access to money from several banks that are willing to lend them money. The money men use money to make money. Many times they use their own money and at other times they use somebody else's money.

If David Richey and his corporate office was opulent, Steve Sachs' office was a little understated. Steve was a second generation investment banker following in the footsteps of his legendary father. This was old money. He had agreed to meet when

I had used my standard line I was going to use on all the insiders. The line was "I was doing a report for an independently large private investment group that was looking at Taser. And I was doing a detailed background work." The fact that they all were so generous with their time just confirmed to me that they were insiders. Any chance to cheer up the company's stock was willingly taken up by the insiders.

I was kept waiting in the posh office of Steve Sachs for over 30 minutes. I was not a client. So I did not deserve immediate attention from the money men. His secretary called me in when Steve was ready for me. He stood up from behind his mahogany desk to give me a handshake. He was in his mid forties. Well dressed. Clean cut. He looked and sounded safe. He had to. He dealt in money. People liked to feel safe when dealing in large amounts of money. He fit the bill. Perfectly. I could see him being very successful. Which he already was.

"How can I be of help?" he was ready to get down to business.

"As you know, I am looking for background information that the newspapers are not covering on Taser. You handled their IPO. So I am looking at a different angle. You were there when Taser was unheard of. How did you manage to raise enough enthusiasm in June 2001 when we were right smack in the middle of the bear market?"

"Well, now in hindsight it looks like we were then right in the middle of a bear market. But if you look back to the charts during the summer of 2001, we had just had a significant market bounce in April and May of 2001. Most folks even thought that we had come to a bottom on the downtrend in the market. After all, the downtrend was by then a year old as the market had topped out in January or February 2000. The public desperately wanted to believe that the down market was over. And it turned out to be a pretty good market to bring new stock in to. Since it was a small offering, we never really needed a big buzz to start. Just a handful of players were involved. And David Richey was quite obstinate in his desire to bring his company to the market by then. He is the client. I can only advise him. But in the end he calls the shots. And it turned out to be easier than I thought to raise the interest in the stock and consequently we were able to raise some money for the Taser IPO through the fall of 2001. Generally speaking the Taser IPO was small by our normal standards and as such did not require too much commitment during its early days," explained Sachs.

"With inbuilt incentives, you must be quite happy with how Taser has turned out," I enquired, knowing that Steve Sachs still held some percentage of Taser's outstanding stock. I just assumed that he had still held onto the stock he was given at IPO as an incentive fee to help distribute the stock.

He confirmed some of it with his answer, "Yes. We did receive, as is the norm, some blocks of shares at IPO as our compensation fee. And at or near today's prices, Taser has worked out well for us. But there is plenty to the upside on this stock. They have tremendous growth. And they are just now beginning marketing into the overseas market. With the cheap dollar they can command a pretty premium in the European market."

And he continued, "But, remember, for every Taser we have half a dozen other stocks that take a lot lot longer to get to our goal and many do not succeed to any extent notable. The IPO is just the beginning. Generally an IPO places blocks of shares in the hands of a few. It is our duty to help full distribution into as many wide and diverse group of holders of stock as possible. Sometimes it takes years and years to achieve that goal. A decade is not unusual to achieve such a distribution. This accomplishes the task we are given by the client at the IPO." At least he was candid enough to let me think that all he said was the absolute gospel. He knew who I was and that with my market insight he did not really offer me anything I did not already know. But I wanted to see him eye to eye. The eyes offer clues that are not usually visible when the conversation takes place on the telephone.

I asked one final and crucial question, "You mentioned that in the early days the financial commitment was small due to the small size of the IPO and the small number of outstanding shares. Nowadays, the stock trades around $200 million a day. It surely requires some more financial muscle to work the stock?"

He knew exactly what I was driving at. I knew perfectly that Sachs was in full swing of setting up the stock for eventual distribution and he had most likely already started his sell out of the overall holdings in

Taser. I knew well that along the move, he had bought at reactions to support the stock and sold into strength at new highs.

All in all, during the course of the past months he had to have had a lot of turnover. Buying more than his intended amounts and selling less than his full holdings. And at some point he had stopped buying at reactions and was now only engaged in selling into strengths. He was now probably holding on to just a small percentage of his holdings and waiting for the new heavy volume strength to sell into. He looked me in my eyes. He saw I knew the game well. I could see the recognition in his eyes. So all he offered was, "We have the ability to use whatever is needed. Obviously at current trading activity levels more is needed than what was needed months ago."

I thanked him for his time. As I headed out of his office, I heard him say into the phone, "You know that earnings release for Taser is set for Tuesday morning."

Suddenly I got the feeling that something was up. I had trouble putting my finger on it right then. It was later that night when I was sitting with Boyd and going over his Taser trades that I understood the full operation that Sachs had undertaken during the past three years on Taser stock. Sachs had started the game three years ago. He had allowed time to let the game be set up fully. He had used his money and connections to support the stock wherever it needed support. He had waited until the market had fully recovered from the bear lows. When most of the market had fully come to a conclusion that the bear lows were long gone, he had started the second phase of his operation. The second phase was to begin a clearly visible solid uptrend on Taser stock. And he was now in the final phase of his operations. He had started the distribution phase and was just waiting for a final close out to end the game.

CHAPTER 6:

APRIL 14, 2004, WEDNESDAY EVENING - THE SPECULATOR'S BASICS

I had just a few of the early notes on Boyd's trading on Taser. He promised he would get me the rest of them before the end of the week. While my second visit with Boyd took less than an hour that Wednesday evening, it took me almost the entire night to put it down on paper. Boyd's trades on Taser exemplified money management and trading techniques.

As an experienced trader I was able to gather the fundamental discipline in his trades. But I had to go over it step by step in my report to Joe. Not because Joe needed the trades explained. But I did not know on whose behalf Joe was working on this report. And

I had to assume that whoever was going to study my report had little stock trading experience. And a novice needed the step by step clarifications and reasoning.

The challenge for me now was to put the trading steps and the discipline and the logic behind every move on paper in a simple, succinct and effective manner. It was not going to be easy. Before I started with Boyd's trades, I had to offer the basics of the trading philosophy. In order to do that, I had to mention the unmentionables. Many of the words I wrote would make the professionals on Wall Street livid. And I would draw their wrath. But I was not a Wall Street insider. I was as outsider of an outsider anyone could be. Had I been an insider, I would never write the report the way I ended up writing it. It would have meant a certain death to my career on the Street as an insider.

Now I had to set the stage before I went into the trades executed by Boyd in any detail. After many attempts, I decided to write the basics of the stock market workings first. This allowed the reader of the report - whether it was Joe or somebody else - the freedom to skip directly to the trades if the reader was well experienced in the way the stock market worked. And I came up with this:

The stock market follows simple rules. The rules of supply and demand fix the price. It is no different from in any other commodity. Stocks are commodities as well. They just have different names attached to them. When demand exceeds supply, prices will rise and vice versa. Contrary to popular belief that buyers dictate stock movements, it is the group of sellers who dictate the stock market. Too many sellers drive prices down and too few sellers will bid up the prices to entice the small number of sellers to sell their holdings. Prices will be bid up to a point where enough sellers will be enticed to sell and convert stocks to cash. Thus, the demand for stocks is filled by the sellers. Essentially sellers control the market on the way down and on the way up. If they withdraw their selling then prices rise and if they flood the market with supplies then prices drop.

Nobody wants to buy a stock that goes down in price. Conversely, everyone wants to buy stocks that go up in price. Logic, therefore, dictates that we should buy a stock that has few sellers if we want a stock that goes up in price. That means to be a successful trader in stocks one must look for stocks that have very little supply. A shortage of sellers will move the prices up. How to find such stocks? Simple - a stock that makes new price highs has fewer sellers. The reason is that when a stock makes a new price high, the stock has entered a price area where it has never been before. As a result, nobody paid a price that was higher than its new price high. Thus, there are no sellers trying to recover their invested funds. Rather, the potential sellers will hold on to a rising stock in anticipation of further higher prices. As a result, there is lack of supply of stock. And consequently this will bid up the prices.

It is a common belief that a company with a sound balance sheet is a good investment. But unfortunately for the general public and those who rely solely on balance sheets, the reality is that the stock market is forward looking. The market moves in anticipation. Not because of what is. Rather, because what will be.

But the insiders on the Street will offer up plenty of services both in research and in tips of stocks that have very good balance sheets. There are more than ample services that tout that they cover the best companies. Best companies in their estimation being companies that have either solid balance sheets or have solid earnings growth. Moreover, the services will offer plenty of add-on premium services with each being pricier than the previous one if you want additional fundamental research. You pay a higher set of fees if you want quarterly earnings and sales data. Add a few more dollars and you will be given the past 15-20 quarters of such data. For a few dollars more you will get return on equity, return on investment, profit margins, estimated earnings for the next four quarters, etc. If you want to spend more for information, some service out there will gladly give it to you. This is after all a capitalistic society. If you want anything, you can get it...for a price. And since one is dealing with Wall Street, the cutting edge in capitalism, one can expect no less than the most sophisticated form of making money. The system is so sophisticated that the circle of insiders is all interdependent and is set up in a manner where no insider can ever reveal to Joe Public what the goings on are.

As has been alluded the stock market's attraction is the promise of riches. That attracts best of everything. Best traders, best analysts, best researchers, best brains, big money, etc. All searching for superior yields. I had asked Boyd that given the smarts in the stock market, how could one hope to beat the market.

His answer was simple. Follow the money. His explanation was that there was no need to research stocks and the balance sheets.

The researchers are researchers and not traders because they are not successful traders. On the street you do what you are good at. If you are good at talking and selling, you are a broker. If you are good at numbers and math, you probably build trading models. If you are a good marketing man, you sell. It does not matter what you sell. It could be research services, stock tip services, brokerage services, mutual funds, hedge funds, etc. Selling is selling. It requires one to be personable, presentable, easy to talk to, easy on the ears and eyes. Selling requires the ability to pursue, persevere, push, pull, play into customers' strengths and weakness and to be persuasive. If you are a good trader, you trade.

The market itself is always forward looking. All the news of the day like the latest economic numbers, interest rates, the actions of the Federal Reserve, etc. was all already anticipated and discounted by the market months ago. That was anticipated and most likely correctly forecasted and already acted upon by the smart money. The smartest folks would do the extra-ordinary research and then based on their research they would act. When they acted, they would act with conviction and with big money behind them. Such action is not discreet. Any astute observer can see it quite plainly. One just has to follow the money. Diligently. How the smart money acts shows up on charts. Charts do not predict. But they will allow us to interpret the goings on. And the clues are visible. The price and volume action on daily and weekly charts offer plenty of clues if one is on the look out for such clues. A stock that is in an uptrend will show clearly a set of higher highs and higher lows with confirming signs offered by volume of trade.

I have seen and come across many who have no faith in charts. To them it is just a bunch of lines on a paper which makes no sense. Others look to predict based on charts. Both approaches are wrong. Charts have but one use. They show if there is heavy buying or heavy selling or nothing going on. Charts can confirm or deny the trend of a stock and the market. They are useful only to those who can interpret them. An x-ray is of no use to the lay person. Its use is only to the radiologist who can read it. A lab report from a medical facility is of no use to the common person and is of immense help to the medical personnel who can read it. A legal conclusion drawn by the courts is interpreted by only those who are trained in legal matters. A mathematics formula is understood and interpreted by a mathematician.

Everything in life is about balance. It is the same in the stock market. Prices settle when there is a balance between the sellers and the buyers. Traders succeed when they have a balance between their understanding of the market, money management techniques and a very clear view of the probabilities. As hard as it is for Joe Public to accept, he learns only through his own terrible experience that buy-and-hold does not work. On the whole the odds are against winning by being fully invested in stocks through complete cycles of bull and bear markets.

Since most folks do not find the easy money or a short cut, they will try for a short duration one method of beating the market or another. It is not by coincidence that there are a dime dozen “beat the market” systems out there. And if everyone was so successful at beating the market, the market as we know it would not exist. Making respectable gains in the market is not easy. It is the market setting a trap when things look easy so that the market can distract us and let us drop our guard and it makes us throw caution to the winds. And then when we are thus set up, the market strikes and takes back much more than what it gave us.

Many have made solid money. But hardly a few have kept it. The vast majority of winners give it all back and more and end up losing to the market in the end. The rare person who wins is the one who has found the right balance between market knowledge, trading techniques, mental toughness, discipline, ability to act in solitude and the ability to be detached from the crowd.

It is not by accident that majority of services and houses will push for diversification. It is marketed as a safety mechanism to protect against weak performing sectors and stocks. Ask any financial planner, adviser or broker. Diversification is the rule. But why would one buy a weak performing sector or a stock in the first place if one knew that in a basket of stocks there will be a few duds?

It proves the point that the service providers on the Street have no clue about the market. And by bringing this to the public's attention only draws the ire and fire of the Street. No wonder one never hears that 85% of fund managers underperform the market. If 85% of the so-called professionals are underperforming the average, why would one let a professional fund manager manage one's money? Is the professional himself invested in his own fund? If the professional was really so good, why does he need to manage other folks' money? Why does he not just manage his own money well and he could be on a sailboat enjoying the sun somewhere?

The best traders are usually unknown because he or she would manage his/her own funds quietly and discreetly. They keep making consistent returns on their money with no need to boast or publicize or market any of their performances. They know that action in silence is the best way to keep on doing what they do best. The market has taught such successful traders the lessons the hard way. As soon as one beats his/her chest of superior performance, the market comes and bites them during a subsequent cycle. Humility is brought to all by the market.

Most folks do not understand the brutality of the market unless they lose big. And even when they lose big, the brutality in the marketplace is lost on most of us. At our best we humans are wonderful beings capable of incredible feats of sacrifice, kindness, generosity and all that is the best in all of us. At our worst humans are capable of unbelievable brutality and cruelty. And since the participants in the stock market are all human, logic dictates we will see the best and the worst of humans there as well. By additional logical extension at its best the stock market can be wonderful in its offerings of incredible riches. And at its worst the market can be incredibly brutal in its punishment. The market has a finality in its hand outs. There are no do-overs. No mulligan. This is not a friendly golf game. Everything is for keeps.

A bad move if not rectified by an immediate exit of the trade will result in a sound thrashing by the market. But a move is only bad in hindsight because every move was initiated as a good move. If one did not think the move was good, it would never have been initiated in the first place. It is bad when the move leads to a crushing loss. And a crushing loss starts off as a small insignificant loss. It then becomes a larger and larger loss. Thus, at some point one has to stop the bleeding from the cut before hemorrhaging to death.

The market hands out its verdict indiscriminately. The market does not care whether one is good or bad, moral or immoral, rich or poor, religious or not, male or female, smart or not, old or young. It only matters if we are with or against its movements. If we are with its movements correctly and then fully invested correctly and perhaps even leveraged with margin on the right stocks, the rewards are immense. And if we are against its movements, the punishment can be devastating unless one acknowledges one's mistake and liquidates all holdings promptly before any serious damage can occur.

CHAPTER 7:

APRIL 15, 2004, THURSDAY MORNING - THE STOCKBROKER

John Romano was third generation Italian. And he had the gift of gab. Whether it was a genetic trait or not, I did not know. His office had all the trappings of a great salesman. Enough elegance with just a little bit of gaudiness to satisfy the old money as well as the new money. John came across as if he was your best buddy. To the older folks he looked and sounded like a son's best friend. He was a salesman's salesman.

Now in his late-thirties, John Romano had seen all that needed to be seen in the brokerage business and more importantly he had done it all. We knew each other reasonably well since we had plenty of common clientele. I had seen him at many golf tournaments held by the insiders of the financial community. Though I was truly an outsider, I would be given passes to some of these events by some of my bigger clients. I would attend some of these tournaments only to maintain my contacts. Over the years I had shared some drinks and chats with John Romano. He was well connected and was a big stock broker in the local area.

As I walked into his office to keep my appointment with him that Thursday morning, he waved me down to a chair across his desk. I read the little sign on his desk. It read: Salesmanship begins when the customer says "No." John Romano was on the phone. He put his speaker phone on to give me a firm handshake and a pat on my back. From the tone on the other end of the phone, it was obvious that John was working his magic on a cold call. He still maintained his daily routine of making a set number of cold calls every morning. This kept him on his feet and on the edge in his sales capabilities. It was a habit he had developed since the first day he walked into the brokerage business over a decade ago.

Cold calls are phone calls brokers make to prospective stock buyers where a sales pitch is made to entice the buyer to buy stocks. These calls are called cold calls as the prospect is picked from a deck of sales leads and is a person unknown to the broker. The typical sales lead comes in the form of a 3"x5" card and has on it all the basic pertinent data of the prospective buyer including but not limited to name, address, telephone number, age, net worth, prior investment experience, etc. And with just a name and a number in hand, the broker is expected to call the lead and make a sales pitch. The best brokers are those who can learn everything about the prospect within moments into the phone call and use that knowledge and human psychology to make a sale.

Truly successful brokers make notes about the prospect and call back in a few weeks or months to follow up. And many times it takes two, three or more such calls to land a sale. John would make his handwritten notes about each call he made. He would write in detail the subject and the summary of the conversation he had with the prospect. He would include anything he learned about the prospect. He would pick up on the prospect's interests, family, current investments, ability to spend cash, sporting interests, personal tid-bits, etc. He would refer to these notes in his subsequent conversations with the prospect. And the prospect would be led to believe that John Romano was his best friend with only the best of intentions. Again, this was a habit he had learned and developed from the old timers when he had started years ago in the business.

As I sat down, I listened with fascination and smiled to myself. I was a spectator to the smoothness and natural ease with which Romano talked to strangers on the phone.

"I am sorry, Bob. I was watching my screen as the shares of Majestic Wireless jumped 5% at the market open today on very heavy volume. Somebody big is buying and buying with some serious conviction," he paused for a moment. "Now where was I?" John said into the speaker phone.

Bob, the cold prospect on the other end of the phone said, "I am not interested in stocks right now. I do not know where you got my name. Please take my name off the list you have. I am looking at real estate at the moment to invest in."

John deflected the skepticism on the phone with casual talk, "Hey, Bob! You and I spoke two or three months ago, remember? You were thinking of real estate even then. I guess you are still looking for the best possible real estate investment. If you recall, I was trying to get you to take a look at shares of Majestic Wireless then. It was a $30 stock at that time. It is now a $50 stock. I am sure you understand that stocks are very liquid. If you want to liquidate stocks to buy your real estate property, all you have to do is call me. I can sell your Majestic Wireless shares at a moment's notice given by you. All I am saying is that while you look around and check out the real estate you have in mind, why let that dough just sit there. I would encourage you to put your money to use. After all, if I had been more effective in convincing you of my recommendation to you two months ago, you would be up $20,000 on a small 1000 share buy on Majestic by now. My research team is pegging a $100 price target on Majestic shares before the year is out. In the past two months it has moved from $30 to $50. The move has just begun," and with that John stopped. He wanted to see what silence would do to Bob. The way Bob reacted in those few seconds of silence would clue in John about how close he was to a sale.

Bob said, "I have never heard of Majestic Wireless." It was a bite. Bob had remembered the name of the stock John had mentioned. Not only the name of Majestic Wireless remembered by Bob, but he had shown interest and the interest was clear in his hesitancy. Bob was asking to be sold on it more.

John complied, "Bob, nobody had heard of Cisco in 1991. Now everybody knows about Cisco. By the time everybody knows about Majestic, it would be time to cash in. The gig is to get in on the ground floor. And get out of the elevator before it reaches the top floor. Take a look around. Everybody has a wireless phone and now the next big thing is wireless internet. Everyone you see walking around with a lap-top or a cell phone or a palm hand-held is going to be on wireless internet in just a matter of time. You are a real estate guy and I do not have to tell you this. You buy low and sell high. You want to be buying before the crowd gets excited and then sell into the excitement."

Bob continued his hesitancy, "I have to think this over with my wife."

John pushed in for the kill, "Ok, Bob. Here is what we can do for you. How about we start off with a small 2000 share lot of a buy on Majestic today? This thing is not going to offer these buying prices for much longer. You can talk to your wife about buying more in the coming days. I'll have my courier pick up your check this afternoon for the 2000 shares of Majestic. He will also have the papers all filled out for you to attach your signature on. By next week your wife will ask you why you did not buy more. So let us get the ball rolling. I'll now switch you to my finance department. They will fill out the forms for you on the phone and courier it for your signature, Ok?"

Bob had no chance. John continued, "Bob, you'll thank me in a few weeks. I'll talk to you again tomorrow once I have your forms and the check. Hold on for a second while I transfer you, Ok?"

Bob was done, "Ok. Thank you."

John put Bob on hold. He turned to the intercom and said, "Suzie. I have Bob on hold. Please help him give you all the information, have the forms fully filled and typed on your computer and arrange a courier delivery for his signature and pick up all at one stop at his home in Scottsdale. Fill in an amount of $100,000 as the amount he will open the account with. Set up the courier for a pick-up this afternoon. Include three of my business cards along with one of yours in the package for him. Thanks."

John Romano turned around and smiled at me. "How are you, buddy? It has been a while," he said. We exchanged pleasantries and we got right to the topic at hand. The Taser stock.

"John. I heard you did some heavy work for Sachs and Sachs on the Taser IPO a couple of years ago. I am doing some follow up work on the Taser story. Basically looking back to see how it all began. Since you were there at the very beginning, I figured you could offer me an angle not covered by the papers," I figured with his salesman's ego, a mention of a possibility of his name being in my report would get him going.

John smiled. He smiled a lot. It was hard to see what was beneath the smile. I did not care what his reason for smiling as long as he could offer me the information I was looking for. His agenda was of no interest to me. I already knew his role in the game. There was little I did not know about the brokerage business. I had been, after all, a reasonably successful commodities broker in my day.

"My friend, I have done some IPOs at the best of markets and others at the worst of markets. Taser was unique. I feel we may be coming to a top on its price run soon. My antenna is up now. And it is saying to me that it is near the top. When Sachs came to me as an outlet for the Taser IPO, I told them that they should go to the boys in New York or San Francisco. But Sachs had been apparently discouraged by those big city boys who were still on the prowl for internet IPOs. Can you believe it? After over a year of thrashing, they were still holding out for internet IPOs. We humans are just amazing. Greed makes us do some really stupid things. Sachs needed to raise a buzz about the new stock but had no outlet. Nobody wanted to touch a gun maker. So Steve Sachs wanted me to sell it locally in the West and in the South to the gun buffs. I told him that a stun gun is not a gun. It needed a different softer sell. I put together a few heavy hitters in the South and in the West who helped support the stock through the fall of 2001. There was nothing to it," explained Romano.

"Surely, you were offered a deal to take up the cause when nobody wanted the stock? And with the way things have turned out, you must have some pretty happy clients," I pursued.

Romano stopped his smile. It was for just a fleeting moment but I caught it and it seemed like I hit a nerve. I knew well enough that I would not get another chance to sit with him on this matter until the stock had fully topped out. And by the time I got to speak to Romano again, my report would have been submitted to Joe already. Romano took a deep breath and then began a story.

"You know how the market works. Nobody in the stock market catches the top of a move. Stocks just keep changing hands from one set of owners to another along their move upwards. I wish my clients had all held onto their shares from the IPO days." He paused to take a sip of water and continued, "When I started selling the IPO on Taser, I had about a dozen heavy buyers who spent a good chunk in supporting the stock through the fall of 2001. They all got their shares at a good price too considering that they all made good money in a short duration of time. About three months after the IPO, 9/11 attacks occurred, Sachs called me and left standing instructions to me that should any of my big buyers wish to cash out of their Taser holdings, he wanted me to call him. Sachs was willing to buy back the stock himself. I called my clients and informed them that a big buyer can absorb their large stakes. Since it was a small stock and traded small amounts, any big sale had to be countered by a willing buyer. Sachs gave me the heads up that he would fill the role of the willing buyer and support the stock's sale price. Most of my clients sold all out of the stock by the end of 2001 or early 2002. Most of my clients had doubled or done better on their money in six months time. They had paid around $6-7/share and had gotten out around $12-15/share. They were happy. Volume was heavy in January 2002 when many big sellers sold but at the same time somebody big was buying as well - I suspect it was Sachs. My clients were happy until the recent few months. Now they see how far Taser has come and they wish they had held on. In fact, now they are looking to get back in at currently ridiculous prices." He paused again to sip his water. He looked at me squarely in the eyes. "It is now over $300 and my clients missed the entire move. And the past two weeks have been amazing as Taser has climbed from less than $200 to over $300 a share. I am now getting more and more calls from them and they wish to buy back in large stakes."

I asked him to recap his conversations with his clients over the past two weeks with regards to Taser.

He replied, "Sure. The past two weeks have been really frenzied. The public is losing its mind. It all began on March 26, when Taser closed up $14.16 a share and closed at $206.94. It had just cleared its prior highs and was into brand-new high territory." He was looking at his charts on the screen now as he was talking to me. He was obviously checking on Taser's daily charts as he was talking. He continued, "It was a brand new closing high and suddenly the public was calling me. They wanted to see what my outlook was. I told them that it was a great stock that had moved from a $5 price range to over $200 in a year. And I did not know how much of an upside it had. But you know the crowd. They were getting excited. The calls began to be a daily development then for me. In the following days Taser made some great daily price gains. Yes, there were some days of very little price movements.

On such days the calls were fewer and shorter in duration. There were no big down days."

Romano continued after sipping on his water for a few seconds, "The one day it pulled back, the calls did not stop. On April 5, the stock pulled back $19.50 and closed at $235.55. It was down from the prior day's close of $255. The calls just kept coming and coming. They wanted to buy but could not figure out where to buy. I could not help much but maintained that the stock was moving up strongly. I just kept saying that the earnings report was due on April 20 and the move may be in anticipation of a good report. But with such volatility it required some hard tough bellies to withstand the whipsaws. In the ensuing days, Taser continued its meteoric rise. The upward moves were mind boggling. The phone calls were getting more and more frequent, and more and more frenzied. Folks started to believe they were missing out on some major move. They all wanted to buy in but were waiting for another reaction. But the stock kept closing higher and higher. From April 6, in four days the stock showed some amazing climb. On April 6 it closed up $41.28 at $276.78. On April 7, it went up again. This time it closed up $17.40 at $294.12. The following day it went up another $5.28 to close at $294.12. And the day before Good Friday it closed that week out at $299.40/share."

John Romano looked up from his screen and sipped on his water again. He shook his head.

And he added, "Oh! I almost forgot. I wanted to tell you that the specialist for Taser on the floor called me yesterday to now inform me that he was willing to sell large blocks if any big buyers show up. The stock specialist for Taser is a guy I know works closely with Sachs. That Sachs - he is something else. I have a suspicion that he is up to something with this Taser thing."

I interrupted him because I had a good idea of what Sachs was up to but I wanted to know what Romano was up to. So I asked him, "I thought you figured the stock was topping. If the big clients want to buy now, are you discouraging their buys?"

Romano laughed, "I am not that crazy. The public wants to buy. I am a salesman. I'll sell them anything they want to buy. I learned long ago that if a buyer believes that a stock is going up, it is my meal ticket and it was my duty to get him to buy what he wants to buy. On the other hand, if he thought that the time was to go short, who was I to disagree and dissuade him? It was his money and he wants to spend it the way he sees fit. I should just facilitate his action without any obstacles. Otherwise, I would lose this meal ticket type large client to another broker who will do what the client wants. The client is the king and the client is always right. If the client sees today's Taser price at $300/share and hears the CEO of Taser touting a $1000/share price, who am I to argue? The client believes the CEO. Not me - I am just a lowly stock broker. Why would I discourage the buy and share my belief that the stock has topped? The buyer will just walk away from me and spend his money with some other broker. In the end, the buyer would still have bought the stock. And I would lose the commissions to somebody else. So I have no interest in dissuading the buyer."

I just smiled on the inside to myself. I had seen this kind of reasoning myself. As a commodities broker back in the 1980s I had encountered the same public mentality. It was just amazing how everything stayed the same, now two decades later.

Romano continued, "This week the stock has pulled back a bit and is trading in the $285-$290 range. The calls have subsided a little this week so far. But today is only Wednesday and we have still two more trading days before the week is out. I can feel it in my gut. By the end of this week or early next week, we may be looking at a price of over $300 a share. And I can guarantee you that I will be deluged by calls from the public as soon as we see a $300 price tag. And the buying interest and frenzy will only increase. They are already feeling like they missed out on a gem. Now they see the prices continue to rise with no reaction in sight. And they will probably see solid earnings reports come out on the 20th. The public will want to be in the stock before that report of good earnings. I can almost see the volume exploding on Monday - a day before the earnings come out. You wait and see."

We continued our chat for a while longer when I received a call from Boyd on my cell phone. He had his complete notes of the Taser trades now available for me. I told him that a courier will come and pick up the material from his home. It was almost lunch time. I decided that during lunch I would call my courier for the pick up from Boyd's house. I took my leave from

Romano's office, expressing my thanks to him for his time.

As I was stepping out, Romano offered a word of advice, "You know, if covered the way I think you will cover this Taser stock handling stuff, you have to make it a fictional story. Otherwise, nobody will believe you and more importantly many insiders in the business will probably ostracize you. You may find that landing new research jobs may suddenly become harder. This is a small world." I was savvy enough to realize that he was right.

CHAPTER 8:

APRIL 15, 2004, THURSDAY AFTERNOON - THE POOL OPERATOR

Pool operators have been around since the time that markets have been around. Nowadays fancy names are attached to them. Hedge fund, managed accounts, etc. come to mind. The name by which they are called today matters only to the regulators. The regulatory paperwork needed varies based on the way the pool operator calls himself. In the end the pool operator does the same thing he has been doing for centuries. He pools funds from several sources into a pot. He then uses the pot to begin, make, use and/or finish a stock's move for the profit of the pool contributors. He uses the pot to trade, manipulate, support or otherwise affect prices of any stock or a bundle of stocks. Some operators also write analysis and sell such analysis to brokers. This is done discreetly and through third and fourth party channels with layers of intermediaries so that a direct conflict is not visible to the wary. But intention to affect and fill a self interest is there, whether by design or not.

Alex Santos was one of the best such operators in the West. His firm - Santos and Holland - was a boutique operation based out of Silicon Valley. He had made his name in the 1990s technology bubble. He had somehow survived the 3-year bear market without losing too many of his customers and subscribers. Which was some accomplishment. His reports were pricey. Lately he had been very good. But the market had bounced from the bear market lows and it was easy to be good. All stocks were moving up.

He had started touting Taser stock heavily the past three weeks. And it had coincided somehow with Taser having doubled its price in the past 5-7 weeks. And I knew there was more to this than meets the eye. At least as far as Alex Santos' personal stakes were concerned. Alex had joined ranks with David Richey in his calls for a $1000 stock price target for Taser shares. I was struck by the exact same price target. I had learned that a few weeks ago Alex had met with the Taser bigwigs and had come away very impressed. And that had followed the latest hype of a $1000 stock price target.

Upon my request, John Romano had made the introduction between me and Alex Santos on the phone that day. I had caught the early afternoon flight to the Bay Area to meet with Alex. He agreed to meet me at a little coffee shop near his office. He was low key and always tried to mix in with the crowd so as not to stand out. It was similar to his operations in the stock market. He tried to make his moves quietly and behind the scenes.

As I picked up my latte and sat down and waited for him, he walked in and sat down across from me. He had a bottle of water with him. He was an average looking guy who would easily pass by without anyone giving him a second glance. He liked it that way. He could operate without calling any attention to himself.

After the small talk about the nice weather in the Bay Area, he began, “I am surprised you decided to fly here to see me. I would have been just as comfortable to offer my views on the phone.”

“I wanted to come and see you since we had not met before. And the folks whom I am working for like to see me earn my fee. For that reason I need to show that I am traveling and meeting with many faces,” I replied. In addition, I had learned that many times it is the unspoken word and the eye contact that offers more information than the spoken word on the phone. It was worth the time and effort to go out and meet him.

“During our conference chat with Romano, he mentioned that you were doing in depth study on Taser. What gives?” he began.

“I am looking at its charts and it is just zooming. I have been retained by some heavy money folks to see what is going on with this stock and what it is that makes this such a hot stock. And I wanted to get a take on it from several different sources. I came across your name since you seem to be recommending this stock highly over the past 2-3 weeks. And I wanted to see what is it that you knew or at least what is that you are willing to share with me about the stock? What makes this such a good investment?"

"I own Taser. So you must know that I will be biased in my view," he generously offered the obvious. He owned the shares. Why else would he tout a $1000 price target on a $300 stock? He was looking for buyers for his intended sale of the block of shares he owned. I knew that now more clearly looking at his face and into those eyes. Like I said, the unspoken word is worth more than the spoken word many times.

"I am surprised that you are shooting for a $1000 price target on a stock that has already risen about 6000% or so in the past 52 weeks. What makes you think such a move is sustainable?" I asked and added, "Some believe the stock is now topping." That last sentence I added did the trick.

He put a straighter face on. And looked directly into my eyes. And confidently stated, "Look, this is a stock that was at $150 just six weeks ago and then people were saying the same thing. That it has moved from $6 to $150 in nine months and that such a move was not sustainable. We have just doubled the price in six weeks. And the move is just beginning as more and more people become aware of the stock and its products. Yes, such moves come around rarely. But this is a rare stock and a rare company with a rare product. The growth has been tremendous. But usually stocks like these make one final solid push for months before selling off. I think the thickest part of the move is just now coming. We may not get to $1000 but I can see an exit at $500-$600 in a few weeks. It is especially completely feasible if the general market behaves well."

"Can I ask you about where you bought the stock?" I was direct.

He was equally candid but I had no way to confirm this but take his word. He said, "I accumulated at an average price of $150 which was near its last 50-day moving average line. It has doubled in five weeks or so. It will double next time much faster as it begins the true move. And then it will collapse. I just need to time my exit right."

"What makes Taser so attractive to you guys?"

Alex looked into his bottle of water. "We are a boutique operation and have about $100 million under active management. Obviously the $100 million is spread over many stocks. Being a smaller operator, we can go in and out of stocks and markets rather quickly and deftly. Far easier for us to do such things than the big boys. So a stock like Taser appeals to us. Since Taser trades about $700 million worth of stock a day nowadays it has enough liquidity for us to be a player."

I had already received the answers I was looking for. More so in what he did not say than from what he had said. So after some additional small talk, I headed back to the airport to catch my return flight to Phoenix Sky Harbor Airport.

I went home to bring my report up to date.

I did not know then. Alex Santos had sold out his Taser holdings on that very day at an average price of $300/share. It would be some months later that I would learn of his sales and the sell out price when his new prospectus would come out listing his winning trades for the first half of 2004. He had doubled his money and that was his way of operating in the market. If he doubled his investment, he would sell out. Especially when the general market was looking as if there was a reaction in progress.

The funny thing is that I noted with interest that his research papers and newsletter subscribers did not receive a sell rating on the stock until May 2004. That was some weeks after Santos had already liquidated his own holdings. But such things are usually overlooked or unnoticed by the general public. Especially when the sell recommendation is distributed via third party channels and there are layers of intermediaries between the analyst and the person making the recommendation to the general public.

CHAPTER 9:

THE SPECULATOR'S BASICS - CONTINUED

Probabilities of wins and losses are the keys to a successful speculative operation. To illustrate the basics it would be useful to start with an analogy to Major League Baseball (MLB). A great ball player bats a .300 average. Similarly, a savvy trader can average three wins out of ten trades and still come out way ahead of the market. His success depends on his trading techniques or money management skills. Most novices will trade all or most of their trading capital on every trade. A truly successful trader starts with a test case entry into his trade. If his test case proves to him that his initial reading of the stock and the market was right, then he will add to his position or make a second commitment. Every step is taken one at a time and is entirely dependent on how the prior move turns out. This is a matter of a lot of experience and skill that comes with time.

As all of us come into the market with different trading capital, different personalities, different risk-reward attitudes, different skills and knowledge, the technique has to be developed by each individual to suit his own personality. But as an illustration, assume we come into the market with a $100,000 trading capital, the first buy would be no more than 20% or $20,000 worth of stock. As we know, cash is king in the markets. Without cash, one has no ability to trade. As much as it is desirable to make significant gains, it is often an overlooked principle that preservation of capital is just as important. Without capital, even the best stock in history will do us no good since there is no capital to trade such a fabulous stock. A key ingredient of preserving capital is the principle of stop-loss. A stop-loss is a pre-determined stop placed as soon as the initial trade is opened to close out the trade should the move turn against us.

The stop-loss arises from the basic fact that we can be either right or we can be wrong in the market. The only way we know we are wrong is if we start taking losses when we should be making profits. It is of no use to us if we stay in a losing position for so long that we lose our trading capital. So we must allocate a certain amount as risk for each trade taken. In order to limit the loss, one must thus place a stop at which point the commitment is withdrawn in order to protect trading capital. Some folks use 8%, and others use 10%.

For ease of calculations, assume we use a 10% stop-loss rule. That means, if once a trade is placed and the move goes against us resulting in a 10% paper loss, an automatic close out of that position is undertaken. For most folks stop-loss is a principle that does not make sense. But ask any successful trader and he will have as his first law of protection against the market some form of the stop-loss mechanism. For our example, we will deal with a 10% stop-loss rule. To illustrate the ability to protect capital and allow oneself plenty of chances to trade, we assume a series of five losses in a row. In our example of starting with $20,000 entry at each trade would lead us after five losses in a row to figures which look like this:

Trade 1 = Entry amount $20,000 10% stop-loss exit leaves us with $18,000

Trade 2 = Entry amount $18,000 10% stop-loss exit leaves us with $16,200

Trade 3 = Entry amount $16,200 10% stop-loss exit leaves us with $14,580

Trade 4 = Entry amount $14,580 10% stop-loss exit leaves us with $13,122

Trade 5 = Entry amount $13,122 10% stop-loss exit leaves us with $11,810

Net trading capital after five losses = $80,000 + $11,810 = $91,810

Or a net loss on trading capital of about 8%.

Now after five successive losses the net capital available for trading has been reduced from $100,000 to $91,810. So for the next five trades, one would calculate the test case entry amount to be 20% of total trading capital or 20% of $91,810 or first test entry for the next five trades would start with an amount of $18,362.

This allows the trader to call his shots many more times in the market. He is looking for that one or two big moves that will more than offset his losses. And when he lands the big mover, he can pack it with all his capital at the appropriate points along the big move. Assume that one lands such a potential big mover, how to add positions to such winners is the next challenge presented by the market. And what qualifies a potential winner to be a winner? Usually a winner will continue its trend and the speed of the trend increases as it approaches the end of the move. For our example, we will assume that we are buying into an uptrending stock.

Usually (but not always), a winner starts off with a quick 20% or more move within the first four weeks of the test buy. Thereafter it boils down to how careful and diligent one is in adding the right amounts at the right time along a potential winning move. It all boils down to how good an interpreter of the stock's chart one is. Some fundamentalists and other balance sheet dissectors will argue against charts. But there is no clearer picture of what is happening in the stock's movement than a clean set of eyes that can read a good chart. A trader who cannot read charts is handicapped and adds to the odds of failing rather than winning. There are those who will point to Warren

Buffet and claim he does not read charts. First of all, what Warren Buffet does or does not do and how he does it or does not do it is an enigma to all. Secondly, there is only one Warren Buffet. But there are many many successful stock traders.

The reason stock charts are important is because through a history of the price and volume action, one can decipher if the smart money is accumulating or not. And if the smart money is accumulating, how and where it is accumulating. A move of significance does not happen overnight. It takes time. It takes time to set up, develop, start, keep up, support and finish out a serious move. It requires a good amount of money and time to accomplish this. And a chart offers plenty of clues if one spends the time and effort necessary to study it.

When big money starts a move after having set up the move, it shows up on the right kind of price/ volume action on the chart. Smart money is the money that consistently makes money. The point being that research of all kinds is available all over the market. But is the research actionable? And if actionable, what kind of action is being shown? Is the action looking like a good amount of money is initiating the move with the right kind of accumulation? And is the move being supported at reactions? All these questions are answered by the chart. When the smart money acts, it acts over time. Usually the set up for the move lasts longer than the move itself. A set up may last years and years and the move may last only 6-8 months. It is not unusual.

Bernard Baruch, the legendary trader, used to say that only liars sold at the top and bought at the bottom. He also said that he would consistently be willing to give up the first 20% of the move before getting in and get out before the last 20% of the move developed. He would be happy with the middle 60% of a significant move.

Each stock has its own personality. Some are volatile. Others are steady. Some change their personalities at different portions of their move. In that respect, stocks are like humans. Each with its own personality. However, most stocks reflect the personalities of the manager of the stock. The manager of a stock is the person whose responsibility it is to set up, begin, support and finish out a stock's significant move and effect complete distribution by the end of the move. The manager is the person at the investment bank or the underwriting company who places the actual buy and sell order on the stock that he is handling. For example, in Taser's case, the manager would be the actual person at Sachs & Sachs who was placing the buy and sell orders in his efforts to effect a full distribution. Which may or may not have been Steve Sachs. Or it could have been one of his more experienced in-house traders.

As a result, it is almost a requirement that by the time the stock is fully distributed into a wide array of holders, it has become headline news. The only reason it is news is because many have become owners of the stock and now it is well known to the public. That is the reason that more the stock is well known, lesser its odds of any significant moves.

Trading is a life long learning experience. And it requires hard work. It requires time. It requires patience. It requires the ability to withstand series of losses. It requires discipline. When folks look for short cuts and easy money, chances are better than even that significant gains are not achievable. In that respect it is no different from mastering any other field of expertise.

I was going to learn much about this from the trade executions effected by Boyd Hunt on Taser.

CHAPTER 10:

APRIL 16, 2004, FRIDAY MORNING - THE SHAREHOLDER, AGAIN

David Richey was busy on Friday. I called him to get his comments to the anticipated frenzy on the new earnings report due on Tuesday. I had to clear away few more questions I had as a follow up. I was put on hold. As I waited, I checked my screen to check on Taser's quote. It was being bid at $340. David could close his positions in Taser and walk away with a cool $170 million stash.

"Good morning. How are you this morning?" David's voice said on the phone.

"I'm fine David. Thank you. How about yourself?"

"I'm great," he replied. I said to myself that it was obvious he was great what with a $170 million wealth. And he continued, "Sorry for the delay. I am very busy today. Everybody wants to know about our earnings report due out Tuesday. I have been fielding calls all morning and I am behind schedule." For someone whose stock made new all time highs, he seemed quite anxious.

"Who are these everybody that you are getting calls from?"

David replied, "You know - the analysts, fund managers, hedge fund managers, newspapers, stock brokerage houses, and so forth."

"How do think your report is going to affect the stock? Can you share where the earnings number is going to be? Will you meet or beat expectations?"

David said, "I am not a stock analyst. The street looks for quarterly reports. I am a long term kind of guy. I took me over a decade to get my company public. I was ten years ahead of the market for my products. I am afraid I cannot answer your questions with any clarity. Plus, even if I knew what the earnings were going to be, it would be inappropriate for me to comment on it."

"Do you follow any stock analysts' comments on your stock? Many have talked to you over the recent past. Are you close to any of these analysts?" I asked.

"No. I do not socialize with any analysts and I do not follow any of them in their recommendations. Any such action on my part may be a conflict of interest," he was quick to point out.

"Do you know Alex Santos? If so, how do you know him?" I took the shot I had to.

"Santos and Holland came to us about three months ago. I gave Alex the tour of the company and the facilities here. That is normal. We do that with many analysts. I have met with him a couple of times since that first tour. But I have not read what he said about us. I avoid such comments from the street to avoid any influence on our own internal analysis of our balance sheet. Alex has spoken to some of our large shareholders. This I know. I have not attended any of his shareholder or analysts' conferences."

"David, how much stock trading experience do you have personally? Have you invested in IPOs in the past?" I was trying to see what he knew about the workings of the market.

"I have the usual experience like most other folks. I dabbled some in the technology stocks of the 1990s. No, I was never involved in any prior IPOs. I have been mostly in mutual funds. And for the most part, I am probably at a breakeven in my account over the past 7-8 years. What I made early on, I lost in the bear market."

I was on my last question for David. "You are worth over $150 million based on yesterday's close. Any temptations to sell out and cash in?" I waited to hear the tone in his voice.

"I am looking for a few more years of great growth. And with it comes stock price appreciation. I do not see myself selling out all of my holdings." I could not believe that he acknowledged he was selling at least some of his holdings. It was hidden in the words in his last sentence when he said, "I do not see myself sell out all of my holdings." Which meant he was going to sell or was thinking of selling a part of his holdings. Again, what is not said is many times important.

I thanked him for his assistance and wished him continued success as we ended our phone call.

CHAPTER 11:

APRIL 16, 2004, FRIDAY AFTERNOON - THE SPECULATOR'S OPERATION

I called my stockbroker after lunch. I wanted to find out some basics about the Taser stock. I asked him if it was possible to short the stock. He replied that the stock was not available for shorting as there was no floating supply available with the broker. When somebody shorts a stock, he is essentially borrowing the stock from the broker and selling it. Thus when the price of the stock in the market falls, the trader can buy it back at a lower price and return the borrowed stock to his broker. The premise is still the same. Only the order of execution has been switched. Instead of buy low sell high, a short trader sells high buys low. But if the broker has no stock to lend to the trader, there is no way to short the stock. I was still thinking about the implications of such a stock shortage. And I took out Boyd's trade records out of my file.

I set aside all my thoughts about the Taser stock shortage and my call to my broker. I set aside everything else I had piled up on my desk. My desk had just two sets of papers on it now. One set was the trade record book from Boyd. These were his notes and trade entries that he journals every time he makes a trade. The second was a set of charts for Taser. This was going to be the tricky part to put down on paper. To coordinate and line his trade entries with the dates on the chart so that the reader could get the idea and the philosophy behind Boyd Hunt's successful trading operations, was not going to be easy.

I set down my notes from my chats with Boyd on the desk beside his trade journal. I did not know how to start. He had started off trading with a test buy of $50,000 on Taser. I looked at his trading record first. It had an order dated October 3, 2003, and it read:

Buy-stop 1500 TASR @$32.68 executed at $32.75

Amount $49,125

Commissions $29.95

Total: $49,154.95

Reason: New all time highs after clearing the Sep 17th new high that was made on huge volume.

On that same day of October 3, he had a journal entry below this first order which read:

Sell-stop 1500 TASR @ $29.68 GTC

Reason: SOP 10% stop-loss (SOP stood for his 'standard operating procedure')

I opened up the Taser chart. And I saw that the stock had made an all time high price on September 17, 2003. It had traded over 1.1 million shares that day compared to its daily average volume of less than 200,000 shares. This was a five-fold volume increase. It was also the highest one-day volume traded on Taser for the most recent 52-weeks. Such a move had clearly signaled some big accumulation had started weeks and months ago and there was a shortage of stock that was going to be created by the big money behind the stock.

Then for about two weeks thereafter, the stock just went sideways without giving back any of the gains it had made in its recent few weeks and months. Thus, the first test buy was made by Boyd as soon a new higher high had been pegged by Taser. And he had placed the order a few days in advance having decided that he would test buy into the stock should it make the new high price. And on October 3, he was filled and he was now in the stock with a test case buy.

He had placed his standard operating procedure of 10% stop-loss. So his notes said, "SOP 10% stop-loss." The sell-stop price was 10% below his buy price. This way the risk he was willing to take on his trade was $4605. This was a predetermined loss he was willing to accept if he was to be proven wrong by the stock and had the stock started to give back the gains, he would have been sold out at his sell-stop price. GTC meant the order was good-till-cancel. The order would stay in effect unless Boyd decided to cancel the order.

The stock started to take off. In just four weeks it doubled in price as it pegged a new high of $69.36 on October 30. The move from Boyd's buy price of $32.75 to the latest new high of $69.36 came in just four weeks and the entire move was without a reaction. This had astounded Boyd as the move had surpassed his expectations. He was now getting aware that he was perhaps seeing the early stirring of a really classic bull run on a stock. Without a reaction to its quick move up, Boyd was unable to figure where and when he could really buy in with a bigger stake.

His first test buy had proven to him that he was right. He was in the right stock at the right time. Now he had to find a place and time where he could place a larger commitment. He figured that if his stock doubled in price in four weeks, then it was just beginning a true move. And he knew there would be at least one pure shakeout move on its move up. So he had to start paying attention to its weekly charts rather than daily charts. Daily charts would probably show many false short-term violent moves that will help eliminate weaker holders of the stock. So he waited for a reaction. The first reaction began in early November of 2003. The reaction took the price down to a low of $51.36. But the reaction was short-lived and by 3rd week of November the stock was back near its prior high prices. Now Boyd was ready to place his larger stake. As the stock came close to its prior highs, he placed the following order:

Buy-stop 2800 TASR @ $69.50 GTC

He was going to buy almost $200,000 worth of additional stock if the stock cleared its prior high of $69.36. He waited. On November 20, he was filled in and he had now placed almost a quarter of a million dollars into Taser. His trade journal read:

Buy 2800 TASR executed @ $69.75

Amount $195,300

Commissions $29.95

Total $195,329.95

He had now 4300 shares of Taser. His average buy price for the 4300 shares was:

(1500 x $32.75 + 2800 x $69.75)/4300 = $56.84

He promptly placed his sell-stop at 10% below his latest buy:

4300 TASR sell-stop @ $63.18 GTC

At worst he would be sold out at $63.18. He still would be ahead since his average price for the entire 4300 shares of Taser was $56.84.

I stopped reading the journal. I flipped out the chart. And I marked the dates and the prices and the stops on it. This would offer clarity to the reader I figured.

TASR continued to run. In a matter of another 3-4 weeks, it marked a new high at $93.48. At this price, Boyd's 4300 shares were worth over $400,000. His investment was a shade under $250,000. He had made over $150,000 profits in about two months time. It would have been easy to cash it in. In fact, it would be natural to most to liquidate the holdings and pocket the gains. But Boyd was a true speculator. Every move was based on what offered the best odds for big wins. The odds in this did not favor selling out. Odds were still tilted toward much higher prices.

As was his norm, Boyd waited for a reaction to the move up to $93.48 to see what clues he could get from the stock. And he got his reaction. The reaction took the stock down to a low of $73.44. This reaction low was still above the price he had bought his large stake at $69.36. After making the $73.44 low, Taser refused to go lower. This only meant much higher highs were in order. After a few weeks of consolidation, the stock started approaching its prior highs again.

It was early January 2004. Boyd decided to play his hand out fully. He waited and waited for stocks like these. And when they showed up, trading them fully through their moves had always paid dividends to him. So he decided to go out on 50% margin if the stock made new highs. Going on 50% margin means that he would borrow up to 50% of his equity from his broker and pyramid the extra borrowed amount on his current holdings. So he ran some numbers. Last high on the stock was $93.48. He decided that the next buy price would be a little above the last high. He would place his buys at a price of $93.75 should the stock clear its old highs and make it into newer, higher highs. So his calculations were as follows:

4300 x $93.75 = $403,125 account value if indeed Taser reached the new buy price

Margin 50% of this amount = $201,562.50

At $93.75, the margin funds will buy = $201,562.50/ $93.75 = 2150 shares

So he added an additional buy stop order to his journal:

Buy-stop 2150 TASR @ $93.75 GTC

And on January 9, his new buy stop was triggered and now he owned a total of 4300 + 2150 = 6450 shares. And as was his standard operating procedure (SOP), he placed his stop-loss as soon as he was filled at the new higher high price. The sell-stop order read:

Sell-stop 6450 TASR @ $85.22 GTC

This was his usual 10% protective stop. He figured if the worst happened, he would be sold out at $85.22. His 6450 shares would fetch him at $85.22 an amount of $549,669. But he owed the margin amount of $201,562.50 to the broker. Subtracting that, he would be left with $348,106.50. Which was still over $98,000 profit over his investment of about $250,000 into Taser.

Taser continued to sizzle and by early February it had hit a high price of $203/share. Again, the temptation was there to sell out at $203 and cash his 6450 shares to collect $1,309,350. And deducting the margin funds of $201,562.50, he could have cleared over a million dollars. But his system of only working after a reaction was pegged, still did not offer good odds at selling out. It meant that still higher prices were due. So he waited for the reaction.

It came hard. This time the reaction was severe and took the stock down to a low of $144.66. This did unsettle him. But when he noted the weekly charts and weekly close, he was confident that this was just classic shakeout - probably the last big correction before the upside move ended. However, from his notes it looked as if he was showing some signs of hesitancy as he placed a sell-stop $2 below this low of that week. He had entered the order:

Sell-Stop 6450 TASR @ $142.50 GTC

And he waited. That was all he could do. His sell-stop never got triggered. The low of $144.66 was the low of the reaction. It was the price volume action on weekly charts that never convinced him of the end of the move. It was the last week of March 2004 when the stock pierced above the $203 prior high and made higher highs. It rose $28 for the week. Now Boyd could feel the end was coming. He felt it would be within days or perhaps within weeks more before the end came for the move. So he started watching the stock closely.

It was unbelievable. He had not seen anything like this in a long time. The three weeks thereafter offered the fastest and most rewarding move on Taser. Boyd just watched in amazement. All the while moving his stop up to a little below the prior week's low. And the moves for those last three weeks are listed:

Week ending April 2, 2004 High $263

Move for the week = +$48.06

Volume for the week = 21 million shares

Close for the week =$255

Week ending April 9, 2004 High $308.22

Move for the week = +$44

Volume for the week = 19.5 million shares

Close for the week = $299.40

Week ending April 16, 2004 High $345

Move for the week = +$42

Volume for the week = 12.5 million shares

Close for the week = $342.30

And then his latest entry entered yesterday read:

Exhaust top is coming and will be here within days. Look for a close with very little percentage change in prices on a daily basis accompanied by the heaviest one day volume of shares traded. On that day sell out near the close of the day.

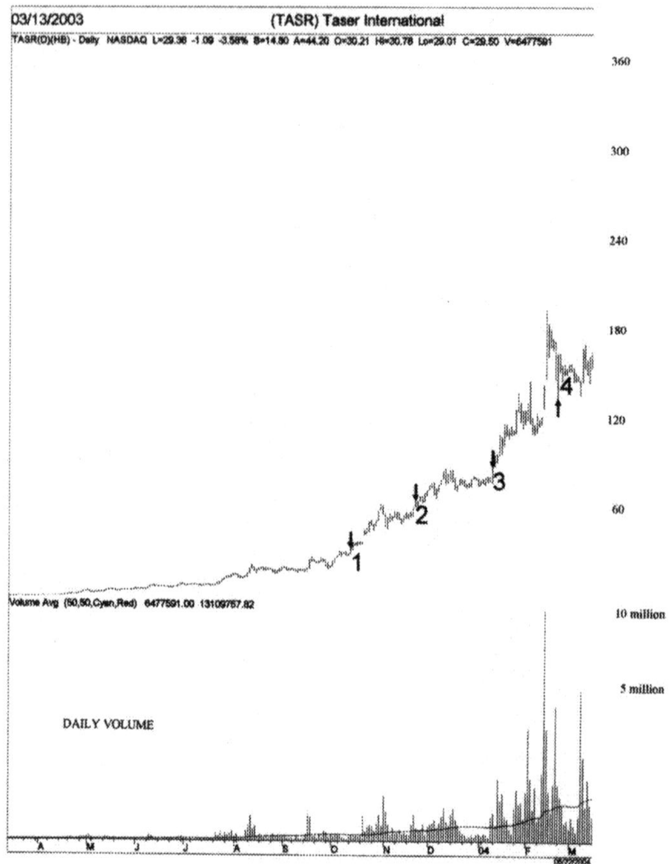

Chart 1. Chart created on TradeStation®, the flagship product of TradeStation Technologies, Inc.

Chart 1 shows Boyd Hunt's trades of accumulation.

1=> Boyd had started off trading with a test buy of $50,000 on Taser. I looked at his trading record first. It had an order dated October 3, 2003 and it read:

Buy-stop 1500 TASR @$32.68 executed at $32.75

2=> He was going to buy almost $200,000 worth of additional stock if the stock cleared its prior high of $69.36. He waited. On November 20, he was filled in and he had now placed almost a quarter of a million dollars into Taser. His trade journal read:

Buy 2800 TASR executed @ $69.75

3 => Boyd decided to go out on 50% margin if the stock made new highs. Going on 50% margin means that he would borrow up to 50% of his equity from his broker and pyramid the extra borrowed amount on his current holdings. So he ran some numbers. Last high on the stock was $93.48. He decided that the next buy price would be a little above the last high. He would place his buys at a price of $93.75 should the stock clear its old highs and make it into newer, higher highs. So his calculations were as follows:

4300 x $93.75 = $403,125 account value if indeed Taser reached the new buy price

Margin 50% of this amount = $201,562.50

At $93.75, the margin funds will buy = $201,562.50/ $93.75 = 2150 shares

So he added an additional buy stop order to his journal:

Buy-stop 2150 TASR @ $93.75 GTC

And on January 9, his new buy stop was triggered and now he owned a total of 4300 + 2150 = 6450 shares. And as was his standard operating procedure (SOP), he placed his stop-loss as soon as he was filled at the new higher high price. The sell-stop order read:

Sell-stop 6450 TASR @ $85.22 GTC

This was his usual 10% protective stop. He figured if the worst happened, he would be sold out at $85.22. His 6450 shares would fetch him at $85.22 an amount of $549,669. But he owed the margin amount of $201,562.50 to the broker. Subtracting that, he would be left with $348,106.50. Which was still over $98,000 profit over his investment into Taser

4=> This time the reaction was severe and took the stock down to a low of $144.66. This did unsettle him a little bit. But when he noted the weekly charts and weekly close, he was confident that this was just classic shakeout - probably the last big correction before the upside move ended. However, from his notes it looked as if he was showing some signs of hesitancy as he placed a sell-stop $2 below this low of that week. He had entered the order:

Sell-Stop 6450 TASR @ $142.50 GTC

CHAPTER 12:

THE CLASSIC POOL OPERATOR

It was not until a few weeks later that I learned about Roger Stonybrooke. And I learned about it from Stonybrooke himself. I knew him from my commodities days. He had been a player in those days and was still a player at his advancing age. And he backed up his plays with big money. What I found was that he was now in a bigger league since he had joined hands with some other players from Las Vegas. Stonybrooke would consistently blow a reasonable chunk of all his market profits in Vegas where he had no chance of winning odds. He did that for one reason alone. It brought him in close touch with other big players. That is how a few years ago Stonybrooke had found acceptable company in Jim Jones and Andre Dulas. Both Jones and Dulas were old money. And they had found Stonybrooke to be a shrewd operator. And had found in him a real market operator like the ones they had never known. Stonybrooke was almost eighty but sharp as a nail. He had seen cycles and cycles in all markets - stocks, commodities, real estate and bonds.

I was at the Scottsdale Fairmont Princess after an early morning round of golf in late May of 2004, when Stonybrooke pulled up beside me. He had heard about my work for Joe on the Taser stock. So he was eager to offer me his take and his play on the stock. Like I said, it looked like everybody who traded in the markets had had a hand in Taser at some point. His story about his involvement in Taser was fascinating.

Stonybrooke recalled that the last time he was at the Fairmont Princess, he was meeting with Jim Jones and Andre Dulas on Saturday, April 17, 2004. It was just 3 days before Taser earnings were due. The three men ordered their drinks and sat down to take a look at some numbers Stonybrooke had scribbled on his notepad in front of them.

Andre Dulas was a recovering alcoholic and the only thing he drank now was water. Jim Jones was downing his beer down with gusto. Roger Stonybrooke was a coffee drinker as long as the sun was up. After sunset he would switch to liquor. It was early evening on that Saturday. Roger was on his umpteenth cup of coffee. The three of them had carried out several successful trading operations in the stock market over the past years.

The brains and the one with the right speculative mind behind the gang was Roger Stonybrooke.

The other two had come to respect the fact that Stonybrooke had an amazing 60% win rate in his market operations. In Las Vegas, where Jim Jones and Andre Dulas operated, such odds of wins were unheard of. A 60% win rate was almost like money in the bank. Especially since the way Stonybrooke operated, he would start any bet with a small pot. So the losses he would take would come on small commitments. Whereas the profits he made would come on large commitments. After the first small commitment he would make and as the bet looked to start to work, he would add to the pot and build up the commitment step by step. Stonybrooke would never accept a loss of more than 10% on the committed funds.

Collectively, the three of them had the ability to call in up to $70 million in combined trading capital if the need arose. For the Taser operation, they were not willing to pool in a pot more than $12 million. This limit was suggested by Stonybrooke based on his take of what the stock could handle in terms of speculative funds without affecting the prices by their trades. So the pool was started with and limited to $12 million with each participant contributing $4 million into the pot.

The plan had begun when Roger Stonybrooke had placed a conference call to both Jim Jones and Andre Dulas in late January. Stonybrooke gave very little details. He stuck only to the common sense part of his proposal. The trade and the chart part of his interpretation he kept to himself. He knew that novices did not understand the message available behind the charts. Stonybrooke's proposal addressed Taser and its products. The market for stun guns was booming in the post 9/11 world. Taser was a virtual monopoly in the field. The stock had run from $30 to over $150 in little over 3 months. This was a stock that was now coming close to its exhaust move or the last part of its move which is usually the fastest and pretty much just straight up for a small duration of time. The move may only last 2-4 weeks but the percentage of move many times runs into triple digit returns.

Roger was an avid chartist. He drew his own charts on a plain graph paper as he plotted the daily open, high, low and close of the stock he followed. He was old fashioned that way. He believed only his own charts. He said any picture drawn by somebody else does not have his own eyes on each and every detail. He had been plotting and watching Taser for weeks and waiting.

He was waiting for two signs. One was that the trade volume reach levels where the $12 million pool money could go in and out without any problems in the stock. And the second sign he was looking for was a clear-cut reaction severe enough to take out most of the weak holders in the stock. He had been watching since October 2003 as Taser continued on a tear from a $35 stock to a $200 stock in early February 2004. On the day that it pegged its high price of $203 in early February, Taser had traded nine million shares. It only had 4.5 million shares outstanding. It would seem on that on one day all of Taser's stock changed hands twice over. Obviously, that was not possible. So what was clearly happening was that a smaller and smaller set of free available shares were changing hands many many times over in a single day. That was a classic sign of accumulation coming close to a point of stock release for eventual distribution. The accumulation had been going on now for several months.

Roger had seen this often enough in his five decades of stock trading experience. The game was the same. Only the players were different. He had started plotting its chart since early January 2004 on his own paper. As the time for action came near, he wanted his eyes clearly on each and every move that Taser made. Then the reaction Stonybrooke was waiting for came in February. His eyes had clearly told him that this reaction was the last one before the exhaust move. The reaction low found support at the stock's 50 day moving average. The 50-day moving average is the line that plots the stock's average closing price of the most recent 50 days. It is just a psychological support line. But if the stock finds support there, it usually means the uptrend has probably not ended. None of the prior reactions had reached the 50-day line. This was the first time it had come down this low. This was it. There were not going to be any reactions now. The next reaction would be the beginning of a collapse.

Roger never committed funds into a position beyond 10 weeks in duration. It was his rule. He only looked for quick moves that would move and end within his 10-week window. His experience of decades had taught him that the big fast moves came always near the end. He was waiting for signs that the move on Taser was coming to an end. And the reaction in February/March had all the classic signs. Plus Taser was trading good volume on an average daily trade by now. It was trading about 1.4 million shares a day. At its price of average about $170 during February 2004, he figured the stock traded on a daily basis over $200 million in dollar value. That was a good volume for him to now look to place his $12 million pool into it. The stock had reached the right volume. Now he was looking for the right buy price. He was looking for the support buy to come in. And it came in near the lows of the reaction of $145. Which is about where the stock's 50 day moving average line was.

So he began his accumulation phase always following up with a 10% sell-stop below his average buy price along the way. His accumulation followed a simple path of adding positions at every $10 price advance. This is the way his accumulation looked:

$1 million spent at $150 share price bought 6600 shares. Sell-stop placed @ $136.

$1 million spent at $160 share price bought 6250 shares. Sell-stop placed @ $141.

$1 million spent at $170 share price bought 5880 shares. Sell-stop placed @ $145.

$1 million spent at $180 share price bought 5550 shares. Sell-stop placed @ $150.

$1 million spent at $190 share price bought 5260 shares. Sell-stop placed @ $154.

$1 million spent at $200 share price bought 5000 shares. Sell-stop placed @ $159.

Total spent $6 million to buy a total of 34,540 shares

Average price $175.00

Selling out target as a stop loss mechanism = $159

But Taser never looked back. So finally when the stock cleared to new highs on March 23, he placed the balance of his bet and bought for $6 million at $204 share price a total of 29,400 shares.

And his final tally was a total of 63,940 shares and he had invested $12 million into Taser. And his new average cost was $187.67/share. In his mind he noted if the stock dropped below $170, he would have to seriously consider starting his liquidation process to protect his capital from serious damage. His entire accumulation phase had lasted 3 weeks.

But as anticipated, Taser just kept moving.

And for the next 3 weeks after his full accumulation, the movements on Taser played out on weekly basis as below. It was surprising to me that his figures were identically written down as Boyd had in his trade journal (the resemblance in these two professional and extremely successful operators did not escape me):

Week ending April 2, 2004 High $263

Move for the week = +$48.06

Volume for the week = 21 million shares

Close for the week =$255

Week ending April 9, 2004 High $308.22

Move for the week = +$44

Volume for the week = 19.5 million shares

Close for the week = $299.40

Week ending April 16, 2004 High $345

Move for the week = +$42

Volume for the week = 12.5 million shares

Close for the week = $342.30

Now the three of them were meeting at the Fairmont Princess on the Saturday after Taser had closed out the week at a closing price of $345 the day before. And Stonybrooke said that at the closing figure of $345, their $12 million invested was now worth over $22 million. And now the time had come to get out and close the positions and to even be aggressive and go short on the stock for a couple or three weeks. He was anticipating a collapse on its earnings report. There was just too much steam built in by now. The steam had to be released. The pressure was to the point of blowing off now.

So he spoke to his partners in the pool operation quietly to see their reaction. He said, "In the next days, I will see a day of volume of trade on this stock that will be the highest volume day. And the instant I see such heavy volume, I will sell into the volume as that will absorb our 63,940 shares. And I would consider immediately going short on about 60-62,000 shares. And I would protect our short position with a 10% stop-loss. This way, the worst that can happen is we lose 10% of our total capital. But with a solid profit on the long positions, we can afford to take such a loss. The upside is that the short move will be quick. And if I am right, we could make a tidy bundle by early May. I am looking at Taser's sister stocks which are other stocks in the security business. And they have all collapsed this week. Taser being the leader will be the last to fall. But it is coming. The time is here. The moment to act will be upon us soon. Very soon."

Andre Dulas and Jim Jones were anxious. This was easy money for them. They did not possess the skills or the patience that Stonybrooke had. Stonybrooke had waited for months and months patiently for the move to develop and come to a steam before placing his commitments. Jim Jones and Andre Dulas were not aware of the months that Stonybrooke had waited for the move to fully develop. He had called on Jones and Dulas only as the time had come close to start the commitments. And when he made commitments, they were slowly built up with protective stops along the way.

Stonybrooke had been devastated by the market a handful of times early on in his career, decades ago. Luckily, Stonybrooke was young, persistent and determined to learn all he could about the market. The few periods of hardships in his youth brought on by the markets had only made Stonybrooke smarter and cautious. But Stonybrooke also knew when to let his commitments have some oomph behind them. And Stonybrooke was not afraid to pack a punch if he felt that the odds were with him.

Andre commented, "Why not add more money to the pot? I mean, if this is as good as it looks to you, we should let the stock have it with some big money."

Jim Jones was also equally vocal and added, "Roger, I see the move you have made the past weeks has turned into a real win. Why not sop it up? I could make a few calls and raise $5 million within minutes on Monday morning."

Stonybrooke looked up from his calculations and his charts. He knew better than to throw caution to the winds. He said, "Fellows. It is one thing to feel the drop coming and to place bets on it. But to load up on bets without a care is another thing. The unknown here is I do not know who else is playing and how big or how savvy the other players are here. They might also play with larger stakes if they see our stakes come into play. There is no sure thing. I am only playing with odds. And I do not wish to give back more than a few percentage points on what we have made. What we have made may look like easy and quick money. But it has taken years and years of learning the hard way. I have big problems with pushing my luck too far. This is about as much risk I wish to take. And I would strongly urge against letting greed get to us. Greed has killed more gains than anything else in the markets. I have seen folks rake in millions over a few months only to give it back and more in weeks. In addition, in the old days I could have called any number of specialists on the floor of the exchange and found out the game being played by some of the big guns. But nowadays the specialists are of a different breed. I do not understand them and they do not understand me. The old kind of specialists are slowly being phased out. It is a new way of operating within the inside. Although, for the outsider, the game has not changed at all. And let us not forget, we are all outsiders riding on the coat tails of the insiders."

Something in the way he said those words felt like an ice cold shower to both Jones and Dulas. So they left the matter in Stonybrooke's hands. They knew that Stonybrooke was the only one among them who had made his wealth in the markets.

Stonybrooke looked at his numbers. He said, "I must say $22 million worth of short sale in the market will need some volume. Especially since we must first sell out our longs. In essence, we are selling almost $44 million worth of stock at one go. This is not done every day on a stock like this. I need to make sure the right kind of volume of trade is available. On top of that I need to look for the open, high, low and closing prices on the stock. Monday and Tuesday may turn out to be big. So I need your acquiescence to closing out the longs and if I see it fit to go ahead and place the shorts. As I said, I will not risk more than 10% of our stock holdings on the short sale. So at worst the total approximate holdings of $22 million we have, will be realized as a $20 million account. Which means that the worst case scenario is that we walk away with $8 million profits on top of our $12 million pot."

Andre Dulas quipped in, "What is the best case you see? Let us say you get out on the longs at current prices. And let us say things play out as envisioned. Where do we cover the shorts?"

"Excellent question. The chart says that current 50 day line is at $216. I would estimate if the heavy selling I anticipate shows up, the first support will be at this price level. Give or take a little. I need to see what kind of support one sees there. Normally on a classic sell-off the down move lasts a few weeks in a row. I would rely more on weekly charts and wait till we see the first up week before buying back to cover the short sale. It is hard to pick a figure. But once I see the sell-off I can answer you better. Today is the 17th of April. I would like to close out the entire operation by 2nd week of May irrespective of how well the short sale works. I do not like long term stakes on a short sale. Best short moves occur rather quickly."

Jim Jones continued his thoughts that indicated no lack of greed, "Do you see any other stocks that look to be setting up like Taser?" He was already thinking of the $10 million or more he could bring in from his bond portfolio for a similar future operation.

Stonybrooke settled that with a cold look and said, "Taser is a move that happens once in many years.

I would be very careful not to be blind sided by one good success in the markets. This is what is called as the perfect stock. Few of them show up in one's lifetime."

Andre looked at the charts and noted with interest that mid-May would be about 10 weeks or so from their first buy started on Taser. Right about the period of time that Stonybrooke usually stayed committed in anyone complete stock operation. Andre marveled at the thinking that went on within the 79-year-old brain of Stonybrooke. The old man had an immense respect from Andre Dulas. Jim Jones was envious of Stonybrooke's ability. Which is a way of showing respect grudgingly.

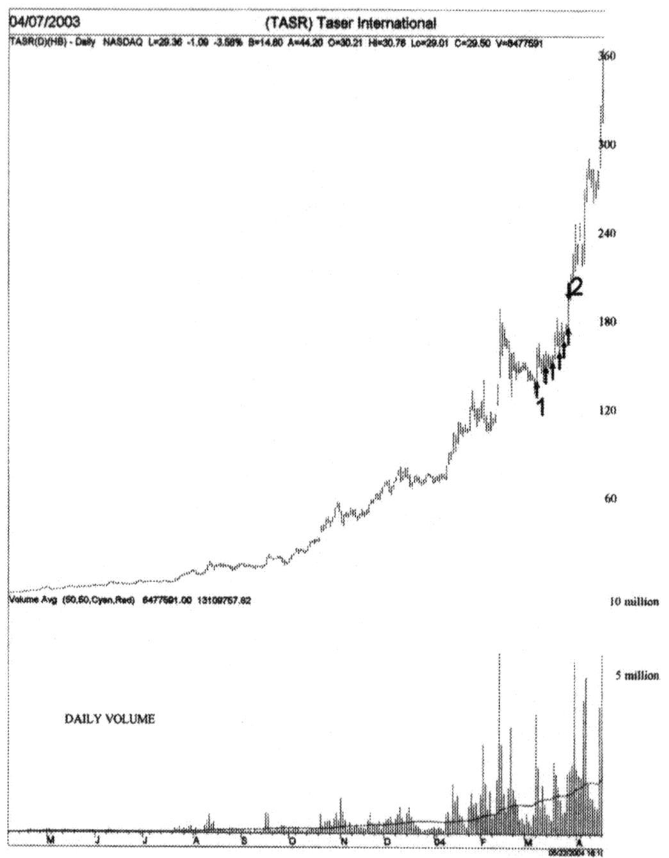

Chart 2. Chart created on TradeStation®, the flagship product of TradeStation Technologies, Inc.

Chart 2 shows Roger Stonybrooke's pool operation on the long side of the trade. He started his accumulation phase right after the stock found buying support around the $145 price level at its 50-day moving average.

1 => Shows that he started his accumulation at $1 million at each $10 intervals on the price up. As the stock moved to $150 after finding buying support near $145, he made his first commitment. Thereafter, he added $1 million worth of shares at each $10 price rise on the stock all the way until it rose to $200.

$1 million spent at $150 share price bought 6600 shares. Sell-stop placed @ $136.

$1 million spent at $160 share price bought 6250 shares. Sell-stop placed @ $141.

$1 million spent at $170 share price bought 5880 shares. Sell-stop placed @ $145.

$1 million spent at $180 share price bought 5550 shares. Sell-stop placed @ $150.

$1 million spent at $190 share price bought 5260 shares. Sell-stop placed @ $154.

$1 million spent at $200 share price bought 5000 shares. Sell-stop placed @ $159.

Total spent $6 million to buy a total of 34,540 shares

Average price $175.00

2=> As the stock cleared to new highs on March 23, he placed the balance of his bet and bought for $6 million at $204 share price a total of 29,400 shares.

And his final tally was a total of 63,940 shares and he had invested $12 million into Taser. And his new average cost was $187.67/share. In his mind he noted if the stock dropped below $170, he would have to seriously consider starting his liquidation process to protect his capital from serious damage. His entire accumulation phase had lasted 3 weeks.

CHAPTER 13:

APRIL 17, 2004, SATURDAY - THE REPORT TAKES SHAPE

I went out to my back patio. It was just after sunset. It had been a long few days for me. I was deluged with stock market and Taser charts in my mind. I had begun writing the report for Joe late last night. I had fallen asleep late at night. When I woke up, it was early afternoon. I grabbed a bite and fell asleep again until just before sunset. My mind wanted to rest. I never argued with my body. If it wanted to sleep, I was happy to comply. I knew I would be inefficient trying to force myself to stay up. And I knew that once I let my mind rest, it would function at peak levels. And hours of my peak mental performance was worth days of inefficient thinking.

I went through a quick recap of the past few days in my mind. I had my notes in front of me. I began writing on my laptop as I sat down listening to the waterfall off the pool. It was a soothing sound to write to. I said to myself that what I knew now was more than what would go into the report for Joe. Joe would get only the facts.

It took me all of the night of Saturday to finish up. After I was done with the report, I stepped into my office. I printed a copy for myself to read. And I emailed the report to Joe. It was 3:00 a.m. on Sunday. I was more than 24 hours ahead of schedule. I knew it was worth more than every penny that Joe would pay me.

Before I logged off, I checked my stock trading account value with my on-line broker. It had $250,000 in cash. After I logged off, I summarized a note to myself. It was written in hand on my yellow legal pad. I addressed it to myself. It said, "If one were a shrewd trader, having made significant gains over the past months, this would be a good time to look into an exhaust run. An exhaust run is when a stock blows off its steam in an incredible move as it tops out after a serious run up. Look for the highest one day trade volume with hardly any gains. That is the first sign to go short. With $250,000 I could probably go short on 700 shares of Taser at current prices of about $350/share."

I decided that this will be my first short trade in many many months. I felt confident. I knew Tuesday was the earnings release date. But the set up would begin before that. Which left only one day of trading - Monday. I could do nothing but wait until Monday.

I stepped back into my back patio and dived into the pool for a swim. I needed to do something physical to take my mind off stocks.

Late Sunday night I picked up my report to Joe and read it to myself to see if I had been mistaken in my outlook. I could not find anything that raised any suspicions. I waited for tomorrow to come.

CHAPTER 14:

APRIL 19, 2004, MONDAY - THE END IS NEAR

Taser's last Friday's close was $342/share. On Monday, Taser opened at $351. It gapped up with early morning heavy volume. It had traded over 2 million shares within the first hour. This was almost half its outstanding shares of 4.5 million shares traded within the first 60 minutes of open. At this rate, it could easily trade over 10 million shares for the day - its highest one day volume ever and over $3 billion worth of money could change hands that day. It looked to be the day of exhaust. It was going to depend on how the stock closed. I turned off my computer. It was no use watching the screen until the last half hour of trade.

I had breakfast. I read the papers. I called my bank. The balance of Joe's payment was in my account. I had made $250,000 in six days. I had to remind myself that Joe probably will make more than that on his Taser trades. There had to be an angle for him to call me and get my work on Taser. I knew it and felt it. I recalled what Boyd had said. The reason for a move becomes clear usually in hindsight. I may have to wait for some time to pass before I would be able to see Joe's angle in all of this.

I checked the quotes on my computer about 30 minutes before close. I was calm. I wrote on my yellow legal pad the details of the trade I had planned for that day. It read:

April 19, 2004 Taser trades

Open $351/share

High $385/share

Low $341/share

Volume at 3:30 p.m. EST - 30 minutes before close = 9 million shares which is its highest one day volume of trade

Current quote $351/share

Change from market open = $0

It fit the bill perfectly. I looked at the notes I had written to myself in the early Sunday morning hours when I had emailed the report to Joe. As I said before, the note said, "If one were a shrewd trader, having made significant gains over the past months, this would be a good time to look into an exhaust run. An exhaust run is when a stock blows off its steam in an incredible move as it tops out after a serious run up. Look for the highest one day trade volume with hardly any gains. That is the first sign to go short. With $250,000 I could probably go short on 700 shares of Taser at current prices of about $350/share."

I placed my order.

Short 700 TASR at market

My screen said;

Executed 700 TASR Short at @ $351/share

I immediately placed the stop-loss:

Buy-stop 700 TASR @ $385/share GTC

This would protect my loss to 10% of my position. That would be the most I wished to risk. Taser closed that day at $356.10. It ended up trading 10 million shares for the day. Well over twice its entire shares outstanding. I closed my computer and walked away.

I called Boyd that evening. I took out my notes from his trade journal. Week of April 12, 2004, was the week that I had been called to work on Taser. And Boyd had written down that the move was likely over as he saw the weekly volume going down as was the percentage weekly move. The collapse was coming. It was just around the corner. He told me on the phone that Monday that he placed a sell as a market order for his entire 6450 shares and was sold out a few minutes before market close on Monday, April 19, 2004. As it turned out he was sold out at $351.

And he had received 6450 shares x $351 = $2,263,950.

Out of this he returned the margin funds $201,562.50 he owed to his broker and was left with $2,062,387.50. He had made $1,817,962.50 on his $244,425 invested. A fabulous return of 744% in just about 6 months.

And in this process, he had proven the point that one needs to trade only a handful of moves a year and wait for the real movers to make big money in the markets. And like Baruch had said, as long as one can grab the middle portion or the meat of the move, one can be very successful in stock trading. It is when we start making foolish attempts to catch the bottom or the top that we set ourselves up for a fall. Boyd had not caught the bottom of the move. But he had caught the fastest and the farthest part of the move which could handle a decent amount of trading capital.

I closed my eyes. And I tried to take it all in. I could not. This is what made Boyd such a successful trader. As I said, he was a rare breed. He is the only one I know of his kind and I know some very successful traders. Boyd Hunt sets himself apart due to his patience and due to his extreme discipline. There are others who use sophisticated mathematical and computer models but they fail as human beings. Moreover, those using mathematic models show way too much turnover and activity in their account which exposes them to many losses. Boyd has no use for any so-called computerized programs. He knows exactly who he is and that is the one thing that keeps him from making too many mistakes.

I called John Romano. I wanted to get a feel from an active stock broker of that day's developments. He took my call but was very short. It had been a very very busy day for him. He had sold tons of Taser stock that day. Many were retail investors. And many were institutions as well. Everybody wanted to buy on that day. But Steve Sachs had sold a very big chunk to help satisfy the buying demand. Nothing he said surprised me. In fact, I would have been very very surprised if it had been any different. Romano asked me to call him back in a couple of weeks when he anticipated to have more time for me and perhaps he could join me for a drink. Everything was falling in place exactly as I envisioned. The ball would start to roll. And roll downward with full speed.

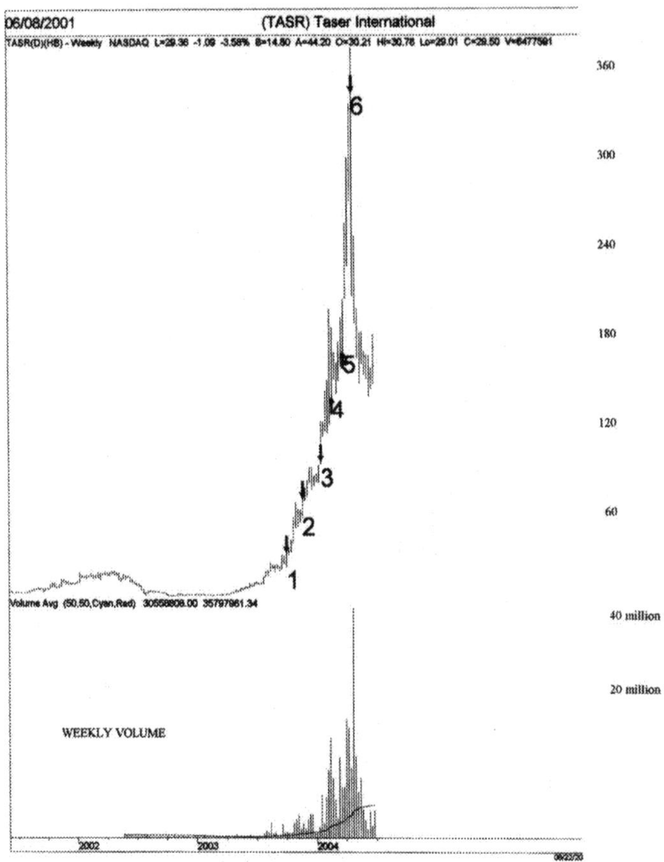

Chart 3. Chart created on TradeStation®, the flagship product of TradeStation Technologies, Inc.

Chart 3 shows Boyd's entire trade on Taser on a weekly chart.

1=> His first test buy where he spent $50,000

2=> His larger commitment of $200,000

3=> His margin commitment of a little over $200,000

4=> The severe reaction came but on weekly chart, the weekly loss was minimal in percentage term and he was confined that this was a last shakeout before the final exhaust run came.

5=> The point at which he started moving his sell-stops to a $1 below the prior week's low price. For four consecutive weeks, Taser made a big weekly positive close. Until it came to the exhaust sale.

6=> Boyd told me on the phone that Monday the 19th of April that he placed a sell as a market order for his entire 6450 shares and was sold out a few minutes before market close. As it turned out he was sold out at $351.

And he had received 6450 shares x $351 = $2,263,950.

Out of this he returned the margin funds $201,562.50 he owed to his broker and was left with $2,062,387.50. He had made $1,817,962.50 on his $244,425 invested. A fabulous return of 744% in just about 6 months.

CHAPTER 15:

SOME OF THE OUTSIDERS

It was the summer of threat in June 2001. At the CIA there was a heightened sense of urgency. Arnie's personal life also took a similar sense of urgency at around the same time. Arnie Schafer was 58. The ringing in his ears had started sporadically 6 months ago. It would come at the most inopportune time. And it would stop just as abruptly as it began. He was fed up with his life. His CIA job had taken him about as far as it could. The new younger brand of crowd in the agency had no use for him.

The ringing in Arnie's ears was getting worse by the day. His wife had just left him. He had just returned to Washington, D.C., after a 2-week holiday he had taken to visit his sick mother in Phoenix, Arizona. In the warmth of the desert, he had found that the ringing in his ears would subside significantly. In his two weeks in Arizona he had just one small episode lasting no more than a couple of minutes. It was not until he was back in his apartment in D.C, that he had realized how nice the feeling of normalcy had been in Phoenix. Within the first hour of returning to his desk at the CIA, Arnie made up his mind. He was going to leave. Right away. Phoenix was beckoning.

Two weeks later in Scottsdale, the upscale suburb of Phoenix, he was hired as head of security for Taser. Taser was the leading stun gun manufacturer in the country. As a signing bonus, he received 2000 shares of Taser. The company had gone public just a couple of weeks earlier.

He checked his dying mother's finances. She had about $25,000 worth of shares in AT&T. He sold it. He was going to put the $25,000 available in her account into Taser. And it would buy him 3500 shares as he added his name onto the account knowing that his mother's days were numbered and that the time needed to make a good return on this investment maybe longer than the time his mother had. Something about the gathering terrorism threat he had seen screaming at him at the CIA told him that the timing was perfect. It was 15 weeks before 9/11 bombings.

Then the 9/11 tragedy hit in September 2001. The stock market was closed for a few days to allow some time for the public to absorb the shock. In a matter weeks, the market had rallied on heavy volume. And Arnie watched in fascination as Taser started to make a move and by early January 2002 the stock was being quoted at over $18/share. He did not wish to push his luck much further. He decided to cash out.

His signing bonus of 2000 shares made him over $35,000. And his and his mother's joint account was credited with $63,000. He knew the move to Arizona was going to be good. It was a good move for him physically as the ringing in his ears had all but stopped. And financially, the move had provided him with a start at trying to build something for himself.

He would be one of the rare few outsiders who made any money on Taser.

Albert Gonzalez had just graduated from the Arizona State University in Tempe, Arizona. Albert was the youngest of four children born to his immigrant parents. He had an excellent math mind and was among the top students in his class right through high school in Los Angeles. In the poor East Los Angeles neighborhood where most young boys grew up with very little education and with few opportunities, Albert's mathematical mind was quite well known. When the Arizona State University offered a scholarship for it bachelor's program, his family knew that this was a ticket for him to get out of East L.A

It was late June 2001. Albert had just graduated with his bachelor's degree. He had gone through several rounds of interviews with Charles Schwab - the leading stock brokerage company. He was waiting for their job offer. In his free time, he waited tables at the bar at the Four Seasons in Scottsdale. The work ethic and the lack of pretensions made Albert a typical hard-working son of immigrants. His folks had migrated from Mexico to Los Angeles in the 1970s.

He had continued his work at the Four Seasons through all of his four years at ASU. It was early evening at the Four Seasons in Scottsdale. Albert was serving drinks to the patrons at the back table in the bar. There were five men. All in very expensive suits and shoes. They were all drinking expensive champagne. At the end of the two hours they were at the bar, their tab was over $1500. It was an unusually big tab for Albert. The tips were very generous as well. Especially for such a small stop at the drinking well.

As Albert recalled, one of them who looked and sounded like a big stock broker, had raised his glass in a toast to celebrate the gathering. The guy who looked like a stock broker had said, “Here is to Taser. The next big mover on the Nasdaq.” That weekend Albert decided to take a look at Taser. He was, after all, a finance major. There was nothing in the company’s balance sheet that struck as unusually solid to him. So he let the matter drop, thinking it was just another stock being listed on the stock exchange.

Two years later in September 2003, Albert was in his Scottsdale office at Charles Schwab. He had now been with Charles Schwab for the past two years since he graduated from ASU. His phone was very quiet that September morning. The stock market was quiet that week. A big stock market rebound after the bear market was in full swing since March of that year. The Iraq war had started and most of the actual war operation was over within weeks. The stock market had taken off from its depressed bear levels. The entire universe of stocks was on a rise.

Albert had received just one call that morning. It was from Boyd Hunt - one of his larger clients. Boyd would trade rarely during the course of any given year. But when he did trade, usually he would pack a big punch trading in decent volumes. It had been many months since Boyd had placed his last trades. Boyd liked to talk to his broker once before he started his trading campaign. Boyd just wanted to maintain his personal contact with a human voice at his brokerage. These days all the action is via the internet and human contact has been lost. In the old days, Boyd had mentioned in his chat with Albert, Boyd would have talked to his broker more frequently. Boyd had started his trades on a stock called Taser International. And he wanted to confirm via phone with Albert that his buy-stop order placed online was received. Since it had been months since the account was active in the market, Boyd wished to get an acknowledgment from a human voice that the online trade was in place.

Knowing Boyd Hunt's prior trading success, Albert decided to study Taser on his own during those weeks. Albert had forgotten that Taser had been on his radar two years ago when he was working the bar at the Four Seasons when he had just graduated from ASU. Now he figured if a successful trader like Boyd took an interest in this stock something of significance should show up there. Albert noticed that the stock had already moved from a $5 stock to a $30 stock. He figured that is a 600% move. The move must be over soon, he thought. Besides the stock looked to be a small cap and very volatile. So he let the matter drop.

He got back to his interests in technology stocks. Albert Gonzalez was like a lot of investors. He had seen what technology had done to the normal everyday life and believed in technology stocks. And he had done what most brokers do. He never took the time to study and learn from his client's wins on Taser. If only Albert had studied Boyd's trades, perhaps he could have learned some very fruitful lessons. But then brokers hardly ever learn the art of successful trading. They are salesmen and make their living selling.

CHAPTER 16:

THE SHORT SQUEEZE GETS SHORTY

The short trader does not own the stock that he sells. So he has to borrow the stock from his broker. To do so, he must place the value of the stock's current price in dollars as a collateral with the broker. The broker then using the cash collateral offered by the trader lends the short trader the stock. The short trader then sells this borrowed stock at current prices. At a later date, the short trader buys back the stock at a lower price and returns the borrowed stock to the broker. Thus the short trader essential sold his stock at a high price and bought it at a low price.

There are two kinds of shorts. Those who are generally successful and those who are generally broken by the market. Just as in the case of traders who generally take the long positions, the successful trader among the shorts is a rarity. There have been almost as many if not more bankrupt short traders as there have been long traders. The only difference between the shorts and the longs is that the successful short move usually occurs quicker and is less rewarding in percentage terms than a successful long commitment.

Shorty Mckenna was a short trader. He had made his share of fortunes and lost it all in the stock market. He had made it all back in 2002 during the worst leg of the 3-year bear market. Beginning in March of 2003, he had taken nothing but losses into the fall of 2003.

Like many short traders, after making good money, he was now going to give it all back to the market. Once again. He had gone through these cycles a handful of times. But he had never stopped to learn about himself and, as a result, he made the same mistakes again and again. Like the majority of participants in the stock market, he did not know that he was his own worst enemy.

Taser did not escape his eyes. He had seen the stock make an incredible run and he was waiting for his view of where the top would be. He had known many such wild runs end in wild drops. He just had not been able to put his finger on a top yet. He waited all through 2003 and the stock just kept making higher highs and higher lows. It was surely in an uptrend. He knew that when the end came, it would be severe and quick. He could not wait.

And in January of 2004, the stock took off upward in what looked like its last breaths. He started to pay close attention to its daily movements. He was sure the top was coming. And when it came, he was going to put his $180,000 of trading capital into the stock on the short side. The stock had yet to violate its series of higher highs. He continued to wait and waited for weeks and months until it happened.

Finally, Taser pegged a high of $146.76 on January 27, 2004. And then it started to pull back a little and pegged a low of $121.50 on the 29th of January. Now Shorty McKenna was ready to make his quick bundle on the stock. All he needed was a clear trade back to a price higher than the prior high of $146.76 and he was going to place his shorts. And the day came on February 2, as the stock hit a high of $154.08. And he immediately placed his line and went short on 1200 shares. His short sale was offered by his broker to him at a price of $149/share. The stock closed that day at a price of $130.80. Shorty McKenna was ecstatic. He had been dead right and with big money on his short sale. He felt very confident. He felt the excitement in his stomach. This was great. He had made over $20,000 in one day and it was on the day of his commitment. He felt it in his bones. He could do no wrong. He was right and he was right on the right stock at the right time. In the coming days the stock would go as low as $117.24. Shorty had seen the stock zoom from $5 about a year ago to now over $150 recently. He felt the drop was coming in a big way. And he would make a bundle. He figured that an upward move from $5 to $150 looked to be setting up at the very least a drop back to well below $100. He knew from experience, that if the stock went below $100, it would encounter a psychological drop further as for humans $100 is a psychological threshold. If broken, usually stocks continue downward further at least for the shorter term. He began salivating. He could not wait. Minutes felt like days and days felt like years.

But something strange happened. Within four days Taser's prices bounced back. Shorty did not know what was happening. This was all wrong. The stock was supposed to head down and continue heading down. He was getting nervous. But he was convinced that this was a temporary bounce. So he could not let go of his commitment. And he watched his screen in horror. It kept going up rather than down.

On February 12, the stock hit a high of $203.22 a share. Shorty was at that price over $60,000 in the hole. He was devastated. He waited till the close and closed out his short position at a price of $180/share. He had lost $37,200 in just eight days. Shorty was mad. He was right. He had felt it deep in his bones. He had over $20,000 profit on the day he placed his line. How could he be so wrong? He felt that the stock was playing with him. He felt sure it was heading down. He could not take his eyes off the screen. For days he was transfixed on the daily quotes on Taser.

Then on March 5, the stock went back again below his prior short sale price of $149 and went to a low intraday of $144.66. He could not believe it. Here it was beginning its down move in full earnest. Once again he felt it in his bones. And once again he placed his shorts. But his $180,000 had gone down to $142,800 after his last short sale loss. So he could only open a line of 950 shares on the short side of

Taser and he got filled at a price of $145/share. It closed at $145.80/share that day. It was a little above his short sale price but he felt confident that this time he was indeed right on the money.

And as the days went by, his confidence was badly shaken yet again. By the time 26th of March came along, the stock was on its upward path once again. Taser seemed to be playing with his mind as if it knew that he was shorting the stock and it was going to teach him a lesson. Shorty was stunned. This could not be happening to him yet again. How can this be? There is not a single stock that moves up like Taser was moving. Now it was approaching $200. This has to be another shakeout. He was not going to cover his short only to be shaken out before the downslide began in all seriousness. How can a $5 stock get above $200 in less than a year? This had to be the end of the move. So he said to himself that he will sit tight and await the stock's top. The top was coming and coming soon, he told himself. But deep inside he also knew that every $1 price rise meant he was losing $950 on his short position. Taser kept on going up. And by the time 6th of April dawned, the stock had reached over $260/share. He had lost over $100,000 on top of his prior losses. Shorty was finished. He closed out his short position at a price of $261/share and received $32,600. In a little less than 2 months his $180,000 was down to $32,600.

Nobody heard from Shorty McKenna after April 6, 2004. What Shorty never realized was that Taser had left many like him in the dust. Many who tried to call its top felt the wrath. Shorty was not alone at all. In fact, he had plenty of company in his misery.

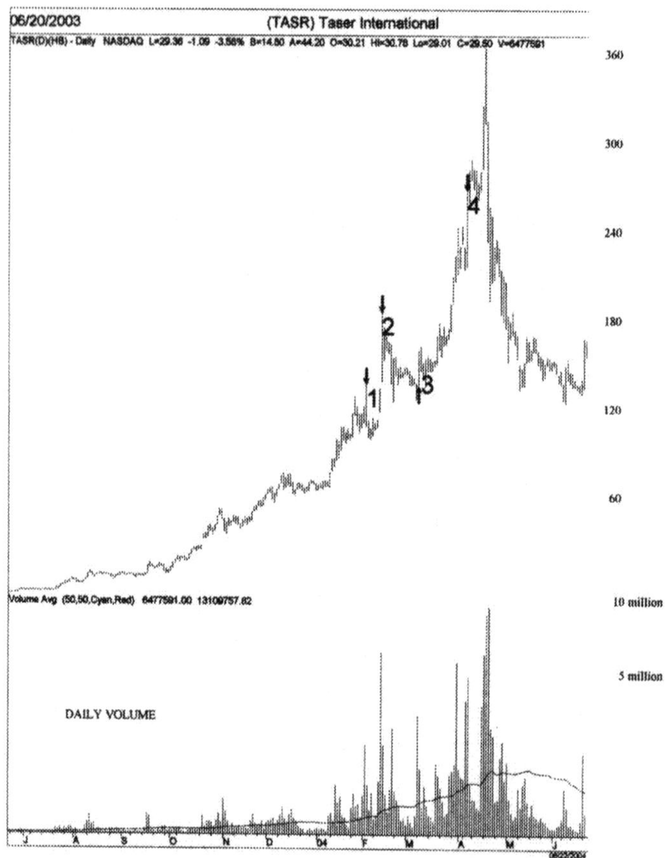

Chart 4. Chart created on TradeStation®, the flagship product of TradeStation Technologies, Inc.

Chart 4 shows Shorty McKenna's short sell trades.

1=> On February 2, as the stock hit a high of $154.08. And he immediately placed his line and went short on 1200 shares. His short sale was offered by his broker to him at a price of $149/share. The stock closed that day at a price of $130.80. Shorty McKenna was ecstatic. He had been dead right and with big money on his short sale. He felt very confident. He felt the excitement in his stomach. This was great. He had made over $20,000 in one day and it was on the day of his commitment. He felt it in his bones. He could do no wrong. He was right and he was right on the right stock at the right time. In the coming days the stock would go as low as $117.24. Shorty had seen the stock zoom from $15 about a year ago to now over $150 recently. He felt the drop was coming in a big way. And he would make a bundle.

2=> Within four days of shorting the stock, it bounced back. Shorty did not know what was happening. This was all wrong. The stock was supposed to head down and continue heading down. He was getting nervous. But he was convinced that this was a temporary bounce. So he could not let go of his commitment. And he watched his screen in horror. It kept going up rather than down. On February 12 the stock hit a high of $203.22 a share. Shorty was at that price over $60,000 in the hole. He was devastated. He waited till the closing minutes of trade and closed out his short position at a price of $180/share. He had lost $37,200 in just eight days.

3=> On March 5 the stock went back again below his prior short sale price of $149 and went to a low intraday of $ 144.66. He could not believe it. Here it was beginning its down move in full earnest. Once again he felt it in his bones. And once again he placed his shorts. But his $180,000 had gone down to $142,800 after his last short sale loss. So he could only open a line of 950 shares on the short side of Taser and he got filled at a price of $145/share.

4=> By the time 26th of March came along, the stock was on its upward path once again. Shorty was stunned. Taser kept on going up. And by the time 6th of April dawned, the stock had reached over $260/share. He had lost over $100,000 on top of his prior losses. Shorty was finished. He closed out his short position at a price of $261/share and received $32,600. In a little less than 2 months his $180,000 was down to $32,600.

CHAPTER 17:

THE WEEK THAT WAS

Earnings report was no longer news because it had been now released before market open on Tuesday, April 20, 2004. It was a very good earnings report. Better than expected. Earnings had risen over 500% over the same quarter of the prior year. The stock opened at $318/share. It had gapped down. Volume was heavy once again. I could see that we were going to see the first clear selling today. Volume was in line with yesterday's heavy volume and yet another day of 10 million share volume of trade was being indicated from the early morning trade volume.

I knew the insiders had set it up perfectly. The entire trading world wanted to trade in Taser. It had become a household name. It was now a stock that the pensioners, housewives, gamblers, day traders, swing traders, long-term investors, retirees, schoolboys, paperboys, the cab drivers, and the elevator men all wanted a part of. It was time, therefore, to supply them with all they wanted to buy and more. And today was the day to help complete the set up that was started months ago by the insiders. The insiders sold with fury. They had more urgency than the buyers did for the first time during Taser's incredible run. The damage was severe that day.

The carnage at the end of the day saw the price drop precipitously as the stock turned over 10 million shares once again. The volume was slightly higher than yesterday's all time heavy volume day. It was the stock's largest one day drop. It dropped a phenomenal $102.90/share. It closed at $252.24. This was a price drop of over 28% in one day.

The public had all bought in yesterday and was being punished today. The public did not know. The pain had just begun. The stockbrokers were busy all day calming their clients. The line was that the reaction was to just a vague perception that the pace of growth was slowing. This was not news. The move had nothing to do with news. In fact, the news was used as an excuse to sell by the smart money.

Next day, Wednesday, April 21, saw the highest one day volume of trade. The stock traded over 11 million shares. It was yet one more volatile session. The stock went as far down to $211.98 at its intraday low. But recovered somewhat and settled at $251.28 - a small loss of $1.92/share for the day. Compared to yesterday, the loss was minuscule. But that was an aberrant support. The clearer view was offered on the weekly chart as one took a look at the trade for that entire week.

The damage for the week read like this:

Volume for the week = 41 million shares

Loss for the week = $98.82

Late Friday of that week, just after the market had closed and Taser had gone through such a phenomenal week of trade, I called John Romano. He confirmed many of my suspicions. Romano had found plenty of willing buyers on Monday and on Wednesday. On Monday, the buyers were mostly people who wanted to be in the stock and were afraid that they may miss out a large move triggered by extraordinary earnings. And on Wednesday, the buyers were mostly folks who thought the fall on Tuesday was unwarranted and were looking for a bargain. And also many who saw a support for the stock at its 50-day moving average. The huge volume of buyers only offered plenty of cover for the big money to liquidate their holdings. And the insiders were all getting out. It was plainly visible to me on the chart. After that chat with Romano, I decided to stick with weekly charts on Taser to figure out where I needed to cover my short positions.

CHAPTER 18: MORE OUTSIDERS

Stu was successful depending on how one defined success. And he was a gambler. He had started many businesses. All failed after some years. But he would escape unscathed through each one of his failed ventures with just enough financial strength to launch his next endeavor. He would chase one project after another without having that extra something called patience. Many of his businesses would have been huge successes if he had only the patience to work a little longer, a little harder and had stuck to them through the rough times. He had the same problem with women. Instead of showing patience and sticking with his wife of 6 years through some rough patches, he launched into a new relationship. And one woman followed another. The gambler in him would chase the riches of the moment and in the process he would miss out on the true treasure.

He had traded his way in and out of many technology stocks in the late 1990s. He had made a lot of money in the stock market. He had given all and more of it back to market during the bear market. The bear market had ravaged him. He was in debt. His silver BMW had just been repossessed. He had already refinanced his house twice.

His trades in Taser stock would be no different. Stu could not help being himself. His biggest obstacle to the pot of gold was that he did not stop to know himself. Stu did not know that in the stock market one must know oneself very well. As a result he repeated his trading mistakes over and over again like almost every other participant in the market. In that respect he was not alone. More than 85% of the humans who get involved with the stock market continue to repeat their mistakes.

Stu found out about Taser's incredible run on CNBC TV on January 1, 2004 as the stock was mentioned as one of the big movers of 2003. It was a show about the best movers of 2003 and Taser qualified. The stock was quoted on the 2nd of January at $85.86/share at its high. On January 5, Stu bought 1000 shares of Taser and paid a price of $85.50/share. Stu wanted some of the action on a mover and a shaker like Taser. He did not have to wait long. Before the end of January the price had run up to $141/share. Stu could not wait. He sold it to lock in the profit. His account had made over $55,000 in less than a month. He was proud of himself.

That weekend he was car shopping. He could now buy a brand-new silver BMW to replace his recently repossessed car. Stu was on cloud nine. But something in him stopped him from buying that car. In hindsight, that was a mistake. He should have spent the money on the car when he had that money.

Stu could not take his eyes of Taser. In mid-February 2004, he checked the price on Taser. He was dumbfounded. The stock was now being quoted at over $200/share. He immediately checked his brokerage account. He had almost $142,000 in his account. The stock had pulled back a little bit and was being quoted at $173/share a couple of days later. The pull back of over $30/share had looked to Stu like a great buying opportunity. He bought 1225 shares at a price $173/share.

He had margined 50% on his account. Which means he had borrowed 50% of his account value from his broker, which was about $70,000 in margin funds. And he was waiting for the stock to go back to above $200/share. But to his dismay, Taser continued its downward move and within days was being quoted at $150/share. Stu got scared. What if the move was over? The Nasdaq had already started to correct and was almost 10% below its high of a month earlier. Stu decided to cut his losses and sold out at $148/share. His account was now down from $142,000 to just a little above $111,000 after having had to give back the $70,000 in margin (borrowed) funds to his broker. He had lost $31,000 in days. He became antsy. Now he was afraid to touch Taser. He decided to keep his money in cash and forget about the stock market for a few weeks.

He received a phone call from a stock broker in April. It was a cold call. It was early April 2004. The stock broker was touting Taser to Stu. Stu was amazed to hear that Taser was now at $258/share. If he had held onto his 1225 shares he would have made a decent gain on it. But now he felt the stock had risen quite a bit fast. And he was not sure that the stock could continue such price moves. So Stu declined the invitation from the stock broker to buy into Taser.

But the call had raised Stu's curiosity. And he started watching Taser's price quotes again everyday. He was astounded. Within 3 days the stock zoomed from $258/share to over $300/share. It was April 15. Tax day. The stock closed at $300/share. The following day the stock closed at $342/share. Stu could not take it any more. There was talk on all the shows about a $1000 price target on the stock within months. On top of this it was releasing its earnings on the 20th of April. That left him with just one trading day before the earnings were released. That was Monday, April 19.

Stu felt desperately like he was missing a sure thing. This was a stock for the ages. He wanted to be a part of the move. It was like the internet days of 1999 once again. He had $111,000 in his trading account. He was allowed to margin up to 50% on his money which meant he could spend $166,500. So, on Monday he placed an order to buy 475 shares of Taser. He paid $350/share and received 475 shares to his account on the morning of April 19. And he waited anxiously for the earnings report that was anticipated to be spectacular.

The following day he woke up late as he had stayed out late the previous night. He checked the earnings report and found it had beaten expectations. The market had just opened and the stock was quoted at $310/share. He thought to himself, the shakeout was once again in effect. After all, he had been shaken out by the stock on a previous occasion, only to see the stock rebound and run on him. So he was going to see how the stock closed.

A few minutes before the close he checked on the price. $255/share. He blinked. How can this be? No, this had to be a joke. He called his broker on the phone to confirm the price. $256/share. He was finished, he thought. It cannot be any worse tomorrow. Surely the stock would come back from such a one day drop. The stock had fallen $102.90/share in one day! This cannot be true. So Stu decided to see what tomorrow brought. He had a terrible night's sleep.

The following day the stock fell yet again. But he gritted his teeth and waited for the close. He was relieved. After going as low as $211.98 intraday, it bounced back to close at $251.28/share. He decided to sit through this severe reaction.

A few days later as the stock continued to drop, Stu finally lost his nerve and closed out his position at a price of $195/share. His account was credited for $92,625 but he owed $55,500 in margin to his broker. And once that was debited, his account was worth only $37,125. He had lost more than two-thirds of his trading capital within weeks. He had made $55,000 on Taser on his first trade in January. But he had lost $105,000 total on his two subsequent trades. He had made a little and lost a lot. Which does not a successful trader make. A successful trader risks little to make a lot. Not the other way around.

Stu was spent emotionally. He was numb. He had it with Taser. He did not want to hear that name again. He had joined the millions before him who had been beaten by the stock market. Stu had never seen a stock like this one. It would be some time before Stu would consider any trading again. He was badly burnt. Again.

He should have bought that Silver BMW when he had the money in his hands.

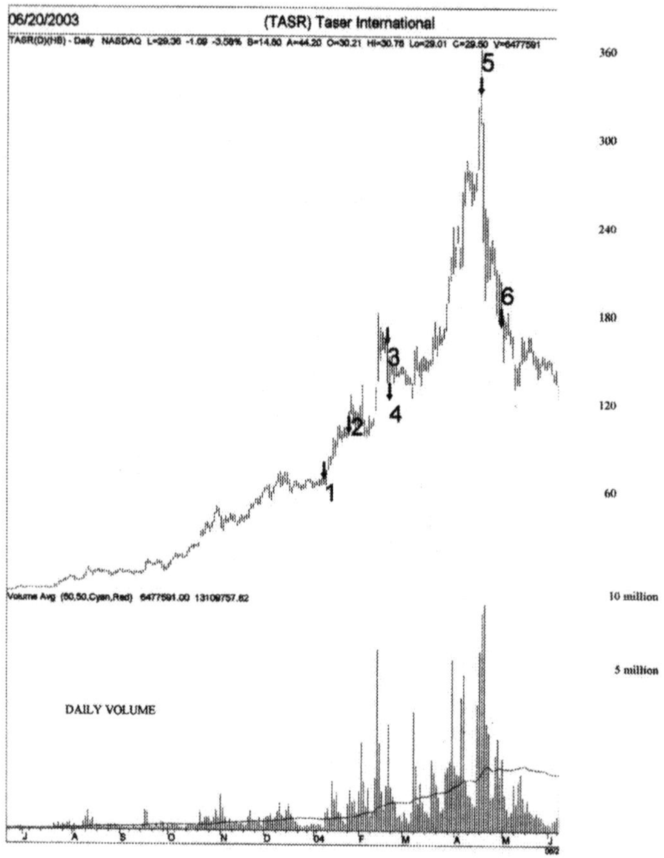

Chart 5. Chart created on TradeStation®, the flagship product of TradeStation Technologies, Inc.

Chart 5 shows Stu's trades on Taser

1=> Stu bought 1000 shares of Taser and paid a price of $85.50/share.

2=>Before the end of January the price had run up to $141/share. Stu could not wait. He sold it to lock in the profit. His account had made over $55,000 in less than a month.

3=> After making a high over $200/share, the stock had pulled back a little bit and was being quoted at $173/share. The pull back of over $30/share had looked to Stu like a great buying opportunity. He bought 1225 shares at a price $173/share. He had margined 50% on his account. Which means he had borrowed 50% of his account value from his broker, which was about $70,000 in margin funds. And he was waiting for the stock to go back to above $200/share.

4=> To his dismay, Taser continued its downward move and within days was being quoted at $150/share. Stu got scared. What if the move was over? The Nasdaq had already started to correct and was almost 10% below its high of a month earlier. Stu decided to cut his losses and sold out at $148/share. His account was now down from $142,000 to just a little above $111,000 after having had to give back the $70,000 in margin (borrowed) funds to his broker. He had lost $31,000 in days

5=> Stu felt desperately like he was missing a sure thing. This was a stock for the ages. He had $111,000 in his trading account. He was allowed to margin up to 50% on his money which meant he could spend $166,500. So, on Monday, April 19, he placed an order to buy 475 shares of Taser. He paid $350/share and received 475 shares to his account on the morning of April 19. And he waited anxiously for the earnings report that was anticipated to be spectacular.

6=>Stu finally lost his nerve and closed out his position at a price of $195/share. His account was credited for $92,625 but he owed $55,500 in margin to his broker. And once that was debited, his account was worth only $37,125. He had lost more than two-thirds of his trading capital within weeks. He had made $55,000 on Taser on his first trade in January. But he had lost $105,000 total on his two subsequent trades. He had made a little and lost a lot.

Bill Kantor was in the hospital for the second time in two years. He had just come out of his second heart by-pass surgery. He was sixty-five and looked at least ten years older. He felt ten years older too. He worked through his pain. And made every effort to sit up. He turned on the TV. They did not have CNBC at the hospital. So he had to settle for CNN. At least he could see the market index numbers on the right hand bottom corner of the TV screen on CNN.

Bill was addictive. It was in his blood. As a young man he had graduated from smoking cigarettes to smoking pot to alcohol. Each addiction was worse than the one prior. In his middle age, he became addicted to the markets. He had made his money in the furniture business. He had opened and made a success out of 14 high end furniture stores in the greater Fort Lauderdale and Miami area. He had been lucky as his timing coincided with the real estate boom of Florida. After twenty years in the furniture business he had sold all of his stores to one of the major furniture chains. Then he made and lost plenty of money in the markets. His addictive personality kept him in one market or the other. He had traded it all - pork bellies, soybean, sugar, coffee, copper, treasury bonds, currencies, silver, gold, stocks, penny-stocks, etc. He was any stock broker's dream client. He would buy any hype.

While his wallet could handle the ups and downs of his trading, his heart could not. He was emotional. Extremely emotional and emotion in the marketplace is a losing proposition. He would be your best friend and the life of the party when he won and an absolute jerk when he lost in the markets. His three ex-wives could attest to his personality when he faced market losses.

He had gone through tens of brokers. Each one was his friend until he lost. He had only one broker now, that he had stuck with through the years. It was Stephanie Rush. She would never pressure any sale. And she had been right more often than wrong. In spite of that, he never made any money on Stephanie's calls because he would always buy too late, sell too early, sell too late or buy too early. Stephanie had warned him on each of his bad moves. But he never listened. She was his center as far as the markets were concerned. She would tell him things as she saw them and she would not hesitate to inform him when she thought he was wrong. Most others brokers would agree with him and would be happy to spend his money. Not Stephanie. In fact, his account with her was the only one on which he had made decent and consistent money in the stock market. But for some reason he never put more money in that account. Bill Kantor was typical that way. Most folks put more money in losing accounts than on winning ones. That was human nature.

He picked up the phone. It was November 2003. The market seemed to be moving up again. He called Stephanie.

"Good Morning, Steph. Bill Kantor here."

"Mr. Kantor. You should be resting and not paying attention to the markets." It was common place in the brokerage business to address clients by first names. It would make the clients feel like they were dealing with a friend. But not Stephanie. She was professionalism personified. She always addressed him as Mr. Kantor. And she kept tabs on his health like a daughter would.

"Well, you know me. I see this thing called Taser is really making a move the past few days. What do you see in it?"

"Mr. Kantor, It is a buy when it clears its next consolidation to a new high. But it is a small stock and volatile and I would go step by step on it," offered Stephanie and she continued, "And as usual I would limit my loss on any buy to about 10% or so."

For a change Bill Kantor decided to follow her lead. He placed a buy-stop order with her for a 1000 shares.

He placed it good-till-cancel. That means the order was in place for 3 months unless it was canceled. And he agreed with her to limit his loss to 10% if his order got filled. He confirmed the order with Stephanie on the phone. He knew all her calls were recorded. It was a protection for the brokerage house that the client had placed the order verbally. Stephanie wrote on her order form:

"Kantor Account Number 2406-2300 order TASR 1000 buy-stop @ 69.47 GTC" and if and when filled "Sell-stop 1000 TASR @ 63.00 GTC as a stop-loss per telephone confirmation by Kantor" and signed her name and date stamped it. It was November 10, 2003. Taser, ticker symbol TASR, closed that day at $59.10.

Ten days later the buy stop was triggered and Kantor's account bought 1000 shares @ $69.50. By the time the New Year dawned, Bill Kantor was exhilarated to see the Taser stock being quoted $85/share. His 1000 shares in Taser was now worth $85,000. Stephanie Rush had been right once again. He called Stephanie to get her read on the stock.

"Hello Steph. Happy New Year. How are you?"

"Happy New Year to you too, Mr. Kantor. I am fine. How is everything?" Stephanie replied.

"Well, I see that the Taser move looks to be working. What do you think if I buy more of it?"

"I think it may be a good idea to do so now. My feel is that we are probably approaching a slowing market in general soon. But there may be one more serious push left on Taser."

Kantor did not need much encouragement. He placed an order to buy another 1000 shares. He paid $86/share. Before long, the stock had made new highs and was being quoted at over $140/share. Kantor started to get itchy fingers and was anxious to cash out. It was early February 2004. He called Stephanie and went ahead with his plan and cashed out the 2000 shares he had in Taser against Stephanie's advice. He received $202/share. It took all he had to control himself. After all, he was recovering from his heart surgery. His breathing lessons were helping a bit. His $155,000 investment was now cashed out at $404,000.

A few weeks later in the second week of April, he called Stephanie yet again. He was screaming, "Why did you let me sell out on Taser? It is now over $300/share!"

Stephanie was used to such ranting and raving from Bill Kantor. He was emotional. A dangerous thing to have in stock market dealings. Emotions have killed more people in the stock market than any other human failing. She tried to calm him down. And spoke with a calm and relaxed voice as she said, "Mr. Kantor. If I recall, it was not my idea to sell out at the price that you did. I was over-ruled by you in that decision. Moreover, I do not believe in being greedy in the market. Greed always comes before fall. Do not forget that you made $249,000 profit on it."

Bill Kantor was hyperventilating by now. He had to flip open his bottle of nitro and take a pill to settle down his heart and his breathing. He sat down. And tried to collect himself. And he said to Stephanie, "I already spent the $249,000 profit I had made in Atlantic City. That is long gone. Now look at what I lost by not holding on to my 2000 shares! I lost an additional $200,000 more that I could have made. Would it be worthwhile to buy it at current levels? They say the earnings coming up next week would be outstanding. The CEO of Taser is talking about a $1000 price on the stock soon."

Stephanie was not wet behind the ears. She had been around the markets for well over a decade and she knew the game. And she imparted the wisdom freely to Bill Kantor and said, "Mr. Kantor, this is not a good time to be buying stocks. Especially a pure momentum play like Taser. Trying to pick the top of a move has left countless people broke."

Bill Kantor mumbled something which sounded like an agreement with Stephanie. Bill Kantor was addicted to the markets. He could not help himself. On April 19, the day before the earnings release he bought back his 2000 shares at a price of $371/share. He did not use Stephanie for this buy. He used one of his other brokerage accounts. He thought highly of Stephanie and did not wish to insult her. He figured that he had asked Stephanie's input and then decided to do the opposite of what she had recommended.

And that would have been insulting to her. Plus he wanted to prove her wrong. He felt he could ride Taser all the way to its $1000 price target. At that price his 2000 shares would be worth $2 million. Kantor could not remove the visions of $2 million from his head.

Four weeks later, Stephanie received a phone from Bill Kantor's brother. He was calling from the hospital. Stephanie was surprised. Bill Kantor had been hospitalized again. He had lost his shirt on Taser. He still held the stock and it was now priced at $156/ share. Kantor's 2000 shares were worth less than $315,000. He had paid $742,000. That was a big loss even for Kantor. Especially so close to his surgery. He was hospitalized as he had developed serious chest pains and he had started having difficulty breathing. The EMS folks had rushed him to the hospital. His heart was in danger of giving out once again. The doctors were working on him. All he had said was, "Taser killed me." Kantor's brother understood Taser to be a stock and had called Stephanie because Bill Kantor had always talked well of her many times in the past. Kantor's brother wanted to know what to do with 2000 shares of Taser that Kantor still held.

Stephanie said calmly that it was best to cash out and stay in cash for some time as the market was showing signs of weakness.

She hung up after the call. She shook her head in disbelief. Kantor had done it again. He had all the right information and decisions made for him and he still did not rely on it. He had gone on to be a victim of his own greed and emotions. And greed is usually a killer in the markets. In Kantor's case, greed truly turned out to be fatal.

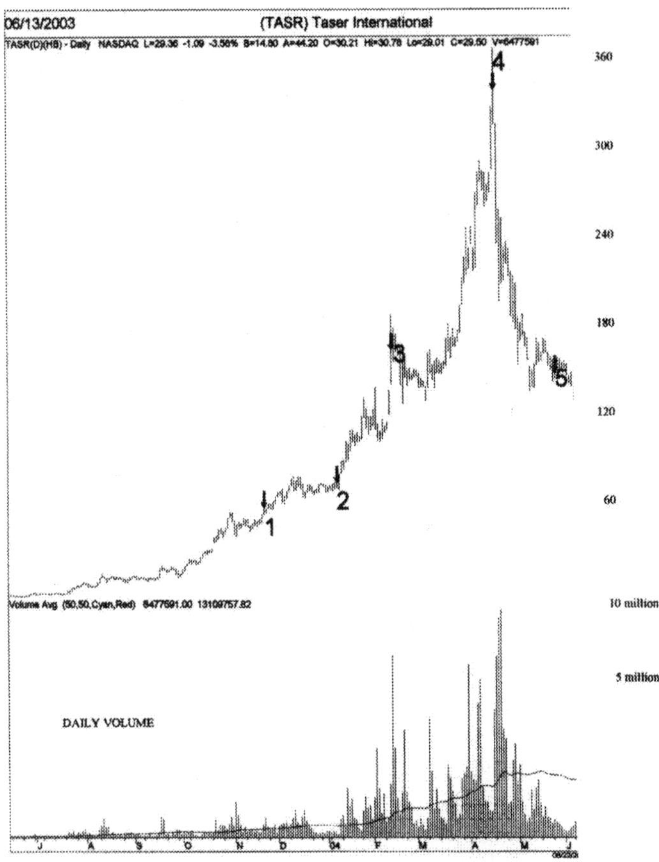

Chart 6. Chart created on TradeStation®, the flagship product of TradeStation Technologies, Inc.

Chart 6 shows Bill Kantor's trades on Taser

1=>Kantor buys his first 1000 shares at $69.50

2=>Kantor buys his second 100 shares at $86

3=> He cashes his 2000 shares out at $202 with a profit of $249,000 on his investment of $155,000

4=> Like the vast majority of the public, he believed that there was not going to be a reaction and the stock would get to $1000 in a straight line up. On April 19, the day before the earnings release he bought back his 2000 shares at a price of $371/share

5=> Stephanie receives a call from the hospital from Bill's brother and she suggests liquidation of all Taser stock

CHAPTER 19:

COVER YOUR SHORTS

It was 4 weeks from the time I had placed by short position in Taser. The quick part of the move was over. I felt it. I looked at the weekly charts and made a notation of the weekly data since the sell off began. I read my hand written data and it read:

Week ending April 23

Weekly Volume = 41 million shares

Price loss/gain for the week = $98.82 loss

Price close for the week = $243.48

Week ending April 30

Weekly Volume = 14.5 million shares

Price loss/gain for the week = $49.38 loss

Price close for the week = $194.10

Week ending May 7

Weekly Volume = 8.4 million shares

Price loss for the week = $21.24 loss

Price close for the week = $172.86

Week ending May 15

Weekly volume = 10.7 million shares

Price loss/gain for the week = $0.06 gain

Price close for the week = $172.92

I saw that the volume had fallen for 3 consecutive weeks from 41 million to 14.5 million to 8.4 million shares. In addition, the pace of weekly price fall had slowed from a loss of $98.82 to a loss of $49.38 to a loss of $21.24. And I noted that for the latest week, the gain was minimal at $0.06. And the exhaust volume was cooling down. So my reasoning was that the fastest and the easiest part of the down move was over. I covered my short positions at the market. I bought back my borrowed 700 shares (short) at $172/ share. I had sold at $351 and bought at a price of $172. On my 700 borrowed shares I had made $125,300 in 4 weeks. Add to the $250,000 I received from Joe, it had been a good 5-6 weeks of work. The best paycheck I ever made on a weekly basis. It was almost $75,000 a week on an average. I knew this was an aberration. Weeks like these do not come around every month or every year for that matter. But I also knew that there were lessons here that I had never learned in the past two decades of trading experience.

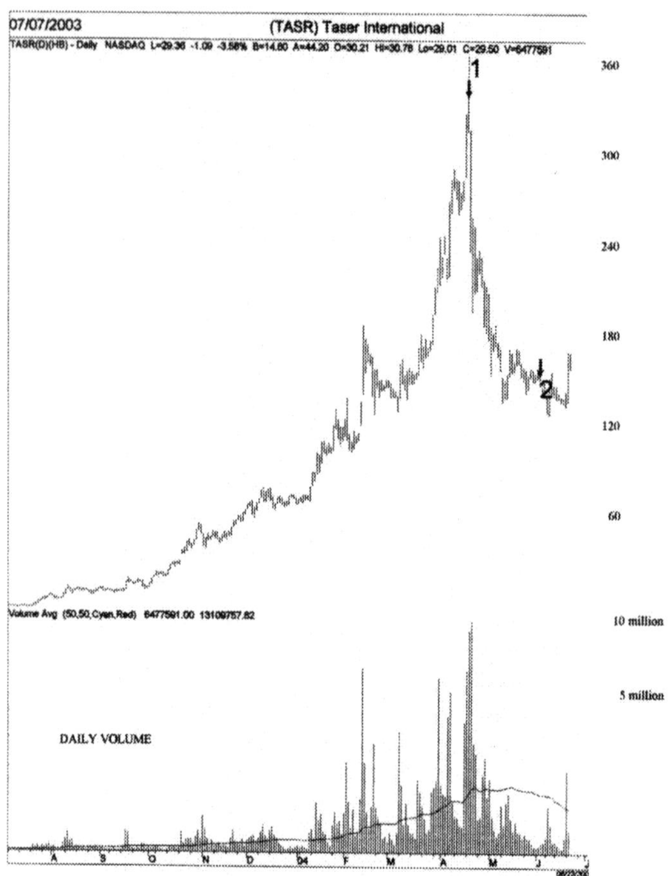

Chart 7. Chart created on TradeStation®, the flagship product of TradeStation Technologies, Inc.

Chart 7 shows my short trade on Taser

1=>I placed my order.

Short 700 TASR at market

My screen said;

Executed 700 TASR Short at @ $351/share

I immediately placed the stop-loss:

Buy-stop 700 TASR @ $385/share GTC

2=> I saw that the volume had fallen for 3 consecutive weeks from 41 million to 14.5 million to 8.4 million shares. In addition, the pace of weekly price fall had slowed from a loss of $98.82 to a loss of $49.38 to a loss of $21.24. And I noted that for the latest week, the gain was minimal at $0.06. And the exhaust volume was cooling down. So my reasoning was that the fastest and the easiest part of the down move was over. I covered my short positions at the market. I bought back my borrowed 700 shares (short) at $172/share. I had sold at $351 and bought at a price of $172. On my 700 borrowed shares I had made $125,300 in 4 weeks.

CHAPTER 20:

WAR STORIES

John Romano met me at the Coyote Grill. I ordered beer for us both. He looked beat. It had been a few long weeks for him. He looked it. He took a few sips of his beer. Like most brokers he could not stop talking. He loved to talk and he was good at it. So it came to him naturally and effortlessly. It was his tool of the trade. The ability to talk well had built a very comfortable life for him.

He continued discussing the brokerage business in general. About how many things about the business had changed over the years. With the advent of the internet and the big bull markets of the 1990s, everybody was suddenly an expert. The public was knowledgeable now about things like P/E ratio, earnings schedules, conference calls, reverse stock splits, earnings per share, stock ratings, etc.

Moreover, the public liked to believe that it was market savvy. While many were indeed market savvy, the vast majority had no clue about successful trading. Most people had some knowledge received from some seminar or from some book they had read. But very few have actual trading experience spanning more than 5 years. By actual trading, John meant where each and every decision to buy, sell, hold, fold and not to trade at all were all made by the individual himself. Where the trader relied solely on himself and nobody else. Where the individual took the time to learn about each of his trades, why the trade was placed, what reasons were listed for the buy/sell, loss-cut, etc. What was learned from each of these trades. What was learned by the trader about himself. What was learned about the market, about the stock, etc. Not many folks spent the time, efforts and energy to study these matters. It is a dangerous thing to know just a little bit of something and to believe that one knows everything.

John Romano was now working on his second beer. He was on a roll. He talked about the old days when he would meet with many of his big clients frequently. He would take them to lunch or dinner and discuss with them his recommendations. He would explain the ups and downs and all things in between. He would call his big hitters whenever he heard or found something new in the market that he thought would appeal to his clients.

Nowadays, he would rarely ever meet face to face with clients. Most of them called him instead and gave him their input about the market or individual stocks. Many would now talk to him in technical terms like

MACD, moving averages, stochastics and such. Some of these terms even Romano had trouble getting the hang of. He asked me what I thought of such technical studies.

I was equally candid with him. I said that most very successful traders who have been around the market for more than a few years have never told me that they found any use for such studies. Usually such studies offer signals that either are too short term of an indicator or are too late or too early and do not in anyway add to one's performance in the market. Besides the services who offer such studies for a price, hardly anybody has made big money on these studies. It may help the scalper make a few points here and there but over time they do not make any serious big money. The big money is made on extremely small number of trades. It is said that for most successful traders 80% of the profit is made in 20% of the trades. Whether that is true or not, I do not know. In my case I do notice that I make big money on a few trades and then hardly any money or sustain small losses on the majority of the rest of my trades.

Romano went on to add that in many other ways, the business had not changed at all. The public still thought that it could beat the market easily. And the belief still was that the stock market makes money for everybody. That is the common myth that most have. Those who beat the market consistently year after year are probably less than 2-3% of the participant population.

If one loosens the criteria and asks how many outperform the market in any given year, the percentage is probably higher and at around 15%. But to repeat the performance year after year is incredibly hard. It requires tremendous discipline and the ability to sit tight without any trades for extended periods of time. This, of course, is almost impossible for most folks to do. The need for action is ever present. The marketing and the machinery behind the markets will never let most humans sit still without any trades. The set up of the move takes a long time. The move itself lasts a small time. Kind of like a horse race. The build up and the set up to train a horse and the jockey takes a long long time. The race itself lasts less than two minutes. Charles Dow used to say if given the patience of six men one could make mentionable returns in the market.

Romano was fast on his drinks. He was on his third beer now. He went on. He said that January was usually a good month for the brokerage business. And as the new year had dawned, he had plenty of interest in the market. The market played out the interest. This was the greatest amount of interest the market had shown in 4 years.

The last time anything close to this kind of appetite was visible to Romano was in January 2000. Just before the market peaked near the end of the bull market of the 1990s. Those highs have yet to be penetrated on the index prices and may yet take years to penetrate. Romano looked back wistfully. January 2004 was also coincidentally when a new wave of heavy buying came into Taser he noted. The volume was pretty active most of the month and toward the end of March the volume of trade on Taser was reaching feverish pitch. He could not place a finger on where the buying and the selling was coming from.

His information from the specialists on the stock did not offer much. He noted the specialists were very discreet and he could not get any information from the trading desks or from the floor in late March. This, Romano suspected, was due to some cooperation between the specialists and the institutional action that the specialists handled. Somebody big was forcing mouths to be kept shut on Taser. Nobody within the trade was able to or was willing to offer any insight. And then the few weeks of mid April came around. The dam burst open. He had such incredible buying interest from the retail end just before the collapse that he heard from his back office that they had problems on Monday, April 19, in closing their books at the end of the day on time. They had to work late into that evening. Trade on Taser during that week was blind in all respects. On Monday, as Taser topped out, the buying was blind greed as every buyer had a $1000 price target in mind on Taser. Everybody wanted in no matter what the price. Then the following day there was blind fear as the stock plummeted. And then buying came back again trying to buy into a bargain. And by the time the week was done volume had exploded for the week.

On that Monday as the stock topped Romano had no need to offer any news to his buyers. They already knew about the stock. But that was not the case the following day as Taser began its drop. On this day Romano had to field many calls about the collapse of Taser's price. He had many who wanted to know why there was such a heavy selling on a good earnings report. Not only was the earnings report good but Taser also announced a stock split coming up in a few weeks. That should have excited the buying crowd. But it looked to add a cold shower on Taser's party.

Besides January being a busy buying month for Romano, April also generally proved to be a busy month year after year. His reasoning was that the early birds would put money into the market at the beginning of the calendar year - whether for tax purposes or whether the optimism of a new year caused it - he was not sure.

And in April the contributions would come in before tax day toward the retirement accounts by the procrastinators. He went on to tell me how he had seen this on Taser as well. In January of 2004, heavy buying came into the stock market and the indices all moved up. It was followed similarly by Taser as Taser pierced to over the $100 price mark. And by the time April came around, Taser was over $300. In fact, he mentioned that it was April 19 - just the 2nd trading day after tax day that Taser topped out at $385/share.

I sat up a little. This was a perspective I had never seen. And I had to marvel at the genius of Sachs and Sachs. Steve Sachs had done the insiders at Taser a great service. He had played the game about as well as I had ever seen. Taser was played by him with impeccable timing.

As Romano and I continued downing our drinks, I mentioned to him that there was a subtle difference between how a stock broker pitches to his potential customers and the way a commodities broker pitches. In many ways the commodities broker had it a little easier because the pitch would be directly tapping into the gambler's mentality.

Joe Public thinks and has the belief that commodities trading is risky and is more of a gamble than stocks. So the job of the commodities broker is easy because he is really feeding the fire of a gambler. The pitch is that one will use only a smaller portion of his trading capital and put it toward the risk of trading commodities. Having set it up in such a fashion, the commodities broker had a further easier job if and when the client lost in the trade because it was already assumed to be risk capital that had a high chance of loss. And the commodities broker then goes back to the client who has just lost some of his capital by trading commodities, and reloads. Reloading is the term that brokers use. It means the broker gets the client to send more money to try and recover the lost money. Since the gig is to appeal to the client's gambling mentality, the job of reloading is accomplished by hype and excitement.

The phone call is full of hype. There is background noise of excessive activity made available by the commission house. There is a feel of hurry and excitement created in the commission house room where all the brokers are housed. The voice of the commodities broker is also excited and full of energy. Minute by minute quotes are interspersed during the pitch. The commission house which runs the commodities account helps foster the excitement within the broker. The idea is that an excited broker will get the potential client excited as well.

In order to excite the broker, the commission house uses many props. Many times there is an in- house pot that is started at the beginning of the week with a large initial donation from the commission house. Every time any broker in the house opens a new account with a client, the commission house would double the pot. And at the end of the week, the broker with the most commissions generated for the house gets the pot. Many weeks the pot would run into thousands of dollars. The incentive is obvious.

Many times the commission house would turn down the air-conditioner so that the temperature was freezing in the office. Cold temperatures would make most brokers to stand up and pace while they talked to try and warm up. And in the process of being frozen due to the low temperatures, the brokers would sound excited on the phones. And the excitement would carry over on the phone to the client. On many occasions the commission house would play loud music before the brokers would get on the phone. The music would be among the many of the latest contemporary party tunes. This would instill a party type happy atmosphere. Again the idea was to get the brokers excited.

The commission house would also offer yearly bonuses to the best brokers. The best broker was defined as the one that brought in the most commissions to the house. It was not the broker who made the most money for his clients. But it was the one who spent the most of the clients' money. With such a system of incentives, the client has no chance of making gains in the market. On the occasions that any commodities trades would make good returns, the pressure from the commission house is to sell out of the holdings with the profits. Then immediately place the now new larger amount of funds promptly into a new position. Thus generating commissions for the house first and foremost. Then at the same time ensuring that a quick spending of the client's money would eliminate the possibility that the client will take the money back since he had profits.

It was common knowledge that a profit making trade would entice the client to spend the money on something. Perhaps a new car. Or jewelry for his significant other. The aim was to prevent the client from spending his money elsewhere and to be fully invested into a subsequent trade promptly. Thus, the ability to take the funds to spend on something else would be taken away from the client. Money is there to be spent. If the commission house did not spend it on trades, the client would spend it on something else. And if the client spent his money on something else, there would be no way for the commission house to earn commissions. Commissions houses are called commissions houses for a reason. They are in existence solely to generate commissions.

The annual bonuses would range from an all expense paid vacation for two to Hawaii to a brand-new car. It depended on the kind of year the commission house was having. Some years were good. Others were better. It was at the minimum always good. That is because there is some commodity that is making some move every year. It may or may not be a tradable move. But the news is made. There were plenty of commodities to trade - including but not limited to gold, silver, copper, coffee, sugar, soybeans, crude oil, heating oil, currencies, treasury bonds, etc. There would be some product that was always making the news. And it did not matter what the direction of the move was. Whether it was moving up or moving down as long as there was movement. And once there was movement and once it made the news - the sales pitch was easy. Hit the client up for money to take advantage of the move that was in the news. There was no need to sell the client. The client was aware of the move from the news. Now the broker's job was to sell the client into spending his money. That was not too difficult as the gambler in the client would be easy enough to be persuaded to take a chance on the trade on the commodity that was in the news.

Many times clients would make an incredible amount of money. Such were the commodities markets. Sometimes the move would be fast and long enough to make a tremendous amount of money. But such moves come about once in many years. If one had the ability to sit and wait for such movements, one can and many do make incredible returns. But to wait for such moves is not possible for most traders. It requires one to be the rare kind of speculator to be successful in the commodities markets.

In such years of decent commodities price movements, the commission house really made it big in the commissions earned. Not because the commission structure was based on performance of the trading account. But because when the client made a lot of money, it allowed the commission house to take the client's hand and make him trade many times over and over again and thus the commissions generated were large. And once the client lost all of his profits on either losing trades or on commissions to the commission house, there was always the recent memory of the big win in the client's mind. That was the hook to hit the client up to send more money into the commission house. The pitch was that it takes money to make money. And to make the kind of big money that was made in the last big winning trade, it takes persistence and large trading funds. The client would more likely than not comply and send additional funds into the commission house.

Now I was on a roll. Like Romano, I was downing my drinks down one after another by now. And somehow his talkative personality seemed to have rubbed off on me. And he was quietly listening to me. Perhaps the long weeks of talking on the phone to his clients had exhausted him. Perhaps he really wanted to hear what I had to say. I do not know what it was but words kept coming out of my mouth with ease. Maybe I felt that he could relate to my rambling since he had just gone through a revealing and exhausting cycle of money changing hands in the stock market where most of his clients had lost or had not made much money even though the opportunity to make a large amount of money had been presented by the Taser stock. Perhaps he was listening because he wanted to be reminded how brutal the market and its players are. I do not know the reason. But Romano lent his ears and I kept talking.

I have seen many of the common goings on of the commodities markets. I knew a bunch of floor brokers on the New York coffee, cocoa and sugar exchange. Back in the days when sugar made a bull run, these guys made huge amounts of money. They had two levels of operations. They had a floor brokerage operation and they had a sister company which handled a retail commodities brokerage operation which would solicit and help trade individual retail accounts.

Legally the two operations were separate enough to avoid regulatory problems that come with such a set up. But from a practical point of view the two operations were more than sisters. They were twins. The set up was simple. They would take their large institutional orders on their floor trade and piggyback them up and down on the retail end. In simple language, assume a huge order to buy is given to their floor trader on the floor of the New York coffee, cocoa and sugar exchange. The floor trader knows that a large order of that size would move the price on sugar a little bit. The move was not much but good enough for many thousands of dollars if acted upon on the futures market since the futures contract was a leveraged instrument. One tick on the price would translate to $11.20 per futures contract on sugar.

So the floor trader would call the twin-sister-operation on the retail end and advise them of the impending large buy. Thus the retail end would place a private buy of their own a few seconds before the floor trader made the big buy on the floor. This trade would be routed on the floor through a third party to avoid regulatory issues. Once the retail buy was filled, the floor trader would then make the big buy on the floor for his big institutional order. The big order would move the sugar price a few ticks. That was all that was needed for the private buy made on the retail end. The retail end would sell out their buy soon after a few ticks of gain. It was a number's game. When done often enough and in large enough figures, the amount of money made was insane.

On top of this, the retail guys started selling a managed account. A managed account is where the power-of-attorney to trade on one's account is given to the account manager. It is a lot like a mutual fund but only the trading is on commodities instead of stocks. And the amount of funds managed is on a smaller scale to avoid regulations. But the premise is the same. The funds are handed over to a trader to trade on one's behalf. And the money raised by the retail end was now following this piggybacking operation. And in the process large amounts of commissions were generated by constant trades. Yes, the managed accounts made money. But the aim was really to generate a ton of commissions by trading 2 or 3 times a day on the managed accounts. With so many accounts and so much funds under management, the commissions generated were massive.

The brokerage business is ruthless. Very few make it and survive and keep their sanity. It is truly a survival of the fittest. The turnover ratio is large. Many last only weeks. The commission house that runs the brokers is even more brutal. It exists for one reason and one reason alone. To generate commissions. The best interests of the account holder is of no consequence to the commission house. In the end everybody loses money in the commodities market.

Since the account holder will lose his money to the market in the end anyway, why not take some of his money as commissions and help delay such a wipe out. The commission house considers commissions as fees paid by the account holder to help delay his losses. Losses are impossible to avoid in the markets but losing all or most of one's risk trading capital had to be somehow justified. Perhaps it is a rationalizing by the commission house. Perhaps they truly believe they are offering a service to the account holders. The point is that the commission house has no incentive to make money for its account holder. And has all the incentives to keep its accounts in one position or another one after another without ever going through periods of inactivity. Periods of inactivity is murder for the commission house. Murder because there is money sitting not earning any commissions and second, the sight of money sitting doing nothing will tempt the account holder into spending it somewhere else with somebody else on something else. And commission generating power of that account has been thus decimated.

The brokerage business has no sympathy. How could it? It deals with and in the markets and the markets have no sympathy for anybody. It is absolutely the jungle of all jungles. Even though the brokers brought accounts into the commission house, the broker himself had no control or any form of 'ownership' on the account. The account belonged to the house. If the broker left the house to work for another commission house, the account stayed behind in the old house. Sure the broker could call the account holder and try and convince the account holder to move his business with the broker to the new house. But there would be plenty of obstacles to achieve that and the task would be so hard that it would be easier for the broker to just try and get brand-new accounts.

Brokers were expected to work and work all the time. Any time when taken off by the broker, whether for R&R or health purposes would be severely punished by the house. The punishment would take on a form of its own law of the jungle. In the absence of a broker, irrespective of the reasons, the house would utilize one of the other brokers and pitch the clients of the absent broker to spend any unspent funds on new trades. If no unspent funds were available, account holders would be encouraged to sell out of one losing position and move into some new positions. Not so much to move the trade to a new potentially better move rather to generate additional commissions. The commissions generated now in the absence of the broker of account, would be shamelessly shared by the house with the broker who was able to convince the account to make new trades. Heaven forbid that such a new trade should make the account some profits. That would mean the account would be now taken over by the new broker who made the trade in the absence of the broker of account. The psychology being that client made money with the new broker and so the new broker can now hit up the client for more money to be sent into the account.

To a broker the move in the market is due to luck or by design. If the move loses money for the client, the broker tells him that it was bad luck. If the move makes the client money, then he is told that the trade was placed by design and the broker takes the credit. Losses are the market's fault. Brokers take responsibility for the wins. It is a beautiful set up.

As we decided to make one last round of drinks, Romano commented that he had a golf engagement with Steve Sachs. And that they were going to talk about some new IPO that was in the pipeline for Sachs and Sachs to handle. The money men were already plotting their next game plan on a new play.

I had had enough for one night. It was getting late that night. Romano and I decided that we should probably continue our chat some other time.

CHAPTER 21:

NO FREE LUNCH

During my early days I had learned that if I am going to lose in the market, I better do it on my own. Why pay somebody else to help me do it? And as funny as this may sound, I found that money can be made in the markets. But it takes a lot of patience, persistence and discipline. And I found that no broker or financial advisor had ever taken the time to learn about successful trading. Most would sell me the line that in the long-run stocks are better investments than bonds. None of them had ever made a fortune trading the markets. But many had made a small fortune selling advice to folks like me. Folks like me wanted to make good money in the markets.

In fact, in my youth I was not unlike many young whippersnappers who wanted to make a living trading. And the real dream was to make a comfortable living at that. And I was a perfect guinea pig for the advisors and the brokers. It all came to me one day when I was a commodities broker in the 1980s. The currency market was in a rally. The dollar was in a longer term downtrend. Many of my clients were making good money trading currency futures and options. I had built them a good line of positions and the market was good. My clients were happy. Then a shorter term correction began.

The commission house where I worked began to play the tricks of the trade. The house started selling the line to its brokers, which included me, that it was time to place half the clients in the long positions and the other half on the short side. I was furious. I was naïve and it was only my first real experience at a true correction in a confirmed trend. And suddenly, the commission house covers its base by placing randomly half its clients on the long side and the other half on the short side? It just flabbergasted me.

I was not alone. There were one or two other brokers who shared my outrage. But the real outrage was that the vast majority of the other brokers had no qualms about this. I was to learn later that such an operation was an age-old well-practiced tradition in most commission houses. Obviously, I cannot paint all commission houses with the same brush. But I found that most brokers knew of such activity. Therefore, by logic it would seem that they had either done it themselves or seen it done.

I and a couple of other brokers quit the commodities brokerage business within days. I made up my mind then to study the markets myself. There has to be a way to make decent money in the markets. Others had done it. So it could not be that hard. Like I said, I was green, young and naïve. Then began many years of losses and many trials and tribulations as I tried each and every method of trading. Nothing I tried worked. Sure I had wins. But no trading system or philosophy ever offered a consistent successful series of outcomes over longer periods of time. I would have wins for some weeks and then the sky would fall. I would give back everything I made and much more. The story was no different no matter what type of systems I used. I took classes here and there. Free ones and expensive ones. And it took years and years. I had by now over five years of failed experiences. Then the light dawned on me. Nobody had a winning system.

The promise of a winning system was just another way of making a living by the sellers of the winning system. I was just one of the many gullible buyers. The free lessons came with added services that were not free. In the end they got my money as well. The free lessons offered the promise of wins. But such wins would only be available if I signed up for at least one, if not more, of the services the lesson giver was offering. And none of the premium services the lesson giver provided were free. In fact, some were downright expensive. This was a sophisticated marketing scheme to extract payment from the gullible public which looked for the promise of fortunes in the market.

I once fell for a service offered by a guy who sold me by touting how he had outperformed the market for 15 years in a row. And apparently for many years he had more than doubled his money. It was only after I paid him did I realize that he would always offer comments like "if you had bought this stock 6 months ago, you would have made twice your money" but he never was able to offer such stocks "before" the move. After the move was over, he would say how the stock met many of his buy criteria. So I tried to find stocks that met his buy criteria before they would make the move. Obviously, to find out what his buy criteria were, I had to fork over more money to him. Of course, it took me some time to get the gig. But by then I was already a lot poorer than when I had started with him.

In the business schools of America where the next set of Wall Street insiders are being trained and the new corporate big wigs will be produced, there are no courses offered on successful trading. There are plenty of courses on corporate finance and more importantly, the leaders of tomorrow are offered plenty of chances to get to know each other.

The contacts and connections made there are more important in the outside world. In business schools the academics talk about something called efficient markets. And a theory called the Random Walk Theory. In simple terms the Random Walk Theory says that since markets are efficient and would reflect the news in pricing mechanisms, stocks take a random walk. And that prices can never be forecasted and will not follow any predictable path.

The professors who teach such courses make the point with an example that should a $100 bill be on the street, one cannot pick it up because in efficient markets somebody already would have the information of the $100 laying on the street and would have picked it up. And thus that a $100 bill is no longer there for one to pick up since it has long gone. The academia which teaches the students in today's MBA programs has very few successful traders. And even if one finds such a successful trader in one of the schools, odds are unlikely that he would ever discuss his trading success to the student body. The reason is simple. To learn the success of trading, one must go through the school of hard knocks in the market by himself. It is a lonely and desolate journey. And there are no short cuts. The lessons may or may not be written in books. But to understand the written lessons, the reader must have experienced the trials and tribulations of the market himself.

In many ways it is not unlike the chats one experiences as a teenager with one's parents. The lessons are offered by our parents but we must still dig our own holes and learn from our own mistakes as teenagers before the lessons make sense. And when we try to impart the same lessons - perhaps in a more up-to-date and hip fashion to our teenage offspring, we find that the cycle kind of repeats itself. We offer the lessons we learned from our own experiences and from our parents to our teen-aged children. But our kids will seldom listen. And more often than not they will dig their own holes and tunnels that they may or may not be able to crawl out of.

The market will extract its tuition. To us traders it feels like losses. Early in one's trading career it feels like a lot of pain. And there is darkness everywhere. Later in one's career, if one is successful and there is a later career, the losses will be smaller. The losses never stop. They just are smaller and more well managed by the successful trader. And they will continue to keep a successful trader on his feet. In that respect, learning the effective trading techniques is a lifelong journey and so is the tuition extracted by the market. Though what the market extracts from the trader will be minimal in comparison to what a successful trader extracts from the market in return.

Ask anyone who has been around the markets for a while and the reply would conclusively be that the Random Walk Theory is just a theory. While it is true that all news is reflected in the stock's price, the fact is at what point is such a full reflection point reached is a big variable. And that is the main cause for market movements and market trends. Again, anyone who has been around the markets knows for a fact that markets go through cycles and through trends. Since such is the case, Random Walk Theory is a just a theory and does not apply in practice. While in the long run, all the news out there is fully reflected in the stock, for the shorter run the stock goes through periods of "anticipating" the news. And it is during such periods that a significant move can be expected. However, once the news is fully anticipated most of the move is finished.

Since in the long run we are all dead, a successful trader is in positions only so long as the trend is in place. And the trend remains in place until it is definitely reversed. There is nothing free in this world. Even more so in the financial markets. If something is free, it is always a set up for a bigger sting to come later. Lady temptation will do her dance until we fall for her. And then just as we get down on the dance floor with full gusto, she will lay the trap.

There is not a single human out there who is right all the time. There is only one participant who bats 1.000 and is right each and every time. Who could bat a 1.000? It is the market. The market is the only one who is always right and never wrong. The market is the collective wisdom of all its participants and therefore, it is obvious that it will be always right. But what is most confounding to me is that nobody takes the time to listen to the market. After all, it is the one entity who will never steer us wrong since it is always right. But we humans want to belong. And we have all the time to listen to other humans but no time to pay attention to the market. Or perhaps we are nothing but ostriches. We bury our heads in the sand and hope the danger will pass away since we think if it is not visible then it does not exist. Perhaps the market tells us of dangers ahead and we do not wish to listen. And we do everything in our power to wish it not to be so. As if by wishing it away, the danger will go away. Perhaps we are all still kids waiting to grow up.

CHAPTER 22:

SOME IDLE THOUGHTS

There is a little kid in all of us. When a kid gets a new toy, an inordinate amount of time is spent by the kid with the toy. Until a newer hipper toy shows up. Now the kid plays with the new toy. Eats with the toy. Sleeps with the toy. This new latest toy is the focus of the kid's life. Gone is the attachment to the older toy. Until a friend starts playing with the older toy. Suddenly the older toy becomes important once again. At the basest level, this is human and animal instinct.

When we grow up, many of the same characteristics show up. Only now the toys are different. To a stock trader it may be the latest, fastest computer with the latest of high speed cable or T1 line fast internet connections. To a gun enthusiast it is the latest model of a gun with the latest technology and mechanisms. To a golfer it is the cutting edge shaft on his irons or the latest golf balls that follow the best trajectories. To a cooking enthusiast it is the biggest and the meanest barbeque equipment. To a car enthusiast, it is the cutting edge mechanisms and high tech gadgets. No matter what one's line of interest, the kid in us is easily excitable.

And the marketing genius in the stock market is about the best. Once again, it is the riches and the promise of riches that brings the best and brightest to the marketplace. We are a capitalistic society. The best will be rewarded financially. So the brokerages all fight to get our business. The best priced stock trade executions. The fastest trade executions. The best fill on a trade. The best online trading platform. The best news service. The best research. And so on…the best of everything is offered to us. And we, like the toy loving kid, will drown in all this excess. And to top it all off, we are offered top tier status if we trade in large volume. The more we trade, the more freebies are offered. And a premium level service is promised. We are suckers. We never realize that the more we trade, the less we have chances to make good money. If I doubled my money on a trade, I could care less if I paid $5/trade or $50/trade in commissions. But no - that focus is taken away from us by the brokers. They sell us on the point that if we make thousands of trades, by getting lower commission rates we will save thousands of dollars in a year. That is just the hook to be attached to the online casino game. And the gambling public will gladly pay more for the chance to lose gambling. A gambler needs an excuse to gamble.

While no two market cycles are identical and no two stock movements are the same, there are enough similarities between the movements to allow one to make decisions and place trades that offer good odds to the trader. The lessons are the same. We just keeping learning them over and over again. Perhaps each time we learn the lessons, we will remember them better. And perhaps each time it is with a lesser tuition payment that we give up to the market as losses than the time prior. But we have short memories. The market knows this and banks on this. And the market will tempt us over and over again into making mistakes. And we will likely end up with some of the same mistakes and some new mistakes. As long as we are wrong small and right big the odds are in the trader's favor.

CHAPTER 23:

THE AFTERMATH

Yet another Memorial weekend had come and gone. It was yet another summer of threat. It was June 2004. Taser was now a distant memory. Those who had started as insiders were now outsiders having sold out of all their Taser holdings with great profits. And those who were outsiders were now insiders since they were the ones still holding Taser stocks and were looking at prices over 30-40% below their buy prices. And it was obvious that after that heavy week of selling in April 2004, the original insiders had stopped paying any attention to Taser. After all, they were now the outsiders and the stock had accomplished its job. They had no holdings and no vested interest in Taser anymore.

I was yet again in cash now after a brief commitment of 4 weeks in Taser stock. It was the one of the shortest periods of commitment I had made which resulted in a decent gain for me. My usual past winning trades placed me in commitments for periods ranging from 8-26 weeks. I was prepared to wait in cash for as long as it took for another clearly trending stock to show up. Anybody who has been around the markets for any reasonable length of time will honestly tell us that more money has been lost chasing returns than anything else. As long as I was in cash, I was not taking any losses. And I had it in me to wait for my wins. While I waited in cash in my trading account, I would be called yet again by some other new client for a report and some digging into some other company and its stock.

And I recalled then that Stonybrooke had closed out his short trades as well. I had to remind myself that Stonybrooke had cashed out his longs at an average of $352 at open on that Monday before the earnings were released. And he had promptly placed his shorts on that same day toward the end of the trade on that day at a price of $355/share. He had liquidated his 63,940 shares out @ $352 and received $22,506,880. That had been over $10 million profit on his $12 million invested in Taser. He had used all his capital available to place his shorts. He was short on 63,300 shares. His short play had lasted only 4 weeks. He had covered half his positions the week after Taser topped out. As he had suspected there had been a first support at the stock's 50 day line. He had covered at an average price of $207/share on half his positions. A couple of weeks later he covered the remainder of his shorts at $170/share. It was the second week of May. From start to finish Stonybrooke had not been exposed to Taser for more than 10 weeks. I was amazed at his skill. His numbers looked like this:

Long 63.940 shares

Average buy price = $187.67/share

Average sell price = $352/share

Profit on longs = ($352-$187.67) x 63,940 = $10,507,260.20

Short 63,300 shares

Average short price = $355/share

Cover 31,650 shares @ $207/share

Profit on this short-cover = ($355-$207) x 31,650 = $4,684,200

Cover 31,650 shares @ $170/share

Profit on this short-cover = ($355-$170) x 31,650 = $5,855,250

Total profits on longs and shorts = $10,507,260.20 + $4,684,200 + $5,855,250 = $21,046,710.20

Or a rate of return of 175% in 10 weeks on his $12 million pool.

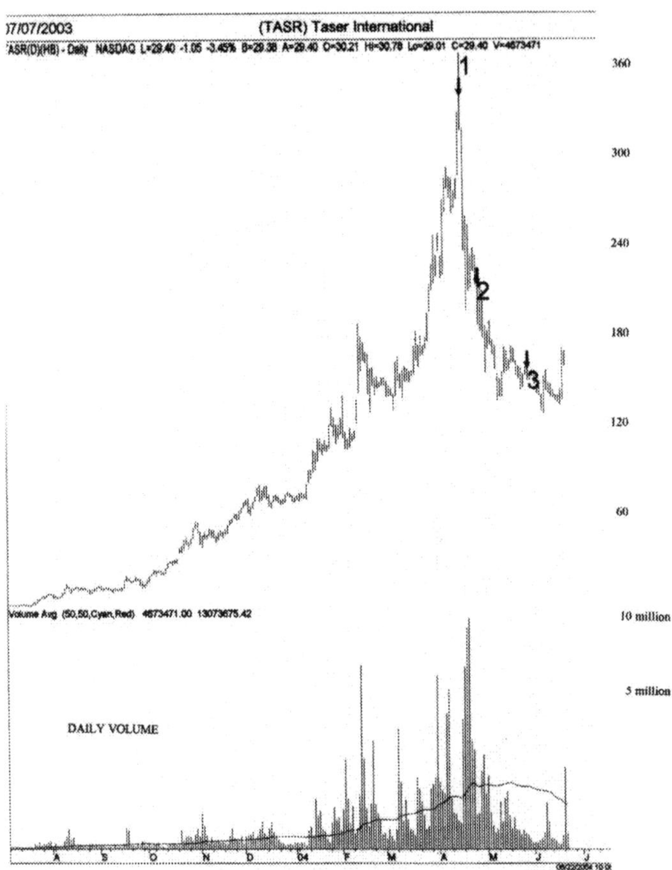

Chart 8. Chart created on TradeStation®, the flagship product of TradeStation Technologies, Inc.

Chart 8 shows Stonybrooke's long liquidation and the short sale operation

1=> On April 19, 2004, Stonybrooke had closed out his longs at an average price of $352/share. And his calculations on the longs showed:

Long 63.940 shares

Average buy price = $187.67/share

Average sell price = $352/share

Profit on longs = ($352-$187.67) x 63,940 = $10,507,260.20

And then he had promptly gone short with the available capital. His short sale price was $355/share.

2=> Stonybrooke covered half his shorts at the 50-day line. And his calculations showed:

Total Short 63,300 shares

Average short price = $355/share

Cover 31,650 shares @ $207/share

Profit on this short-cover = ($355-$207) x 31,650 = $4,684,200

3=> He covers the balance of his shorts. It was the second week of May. From start to finish Stonybrooke had not been exposed to Taser for more than 10 weeks.

Cover 31,650 shares @ $170/share

Profit on this short-cover = ($355-$170) x 31,650 = $5,855,250

And he had made over 174% return on his $12 million invested within 10 weeks.

It was then that I decided to write my experiences of those few weeks. I knew the lessons would be my ticket for the rest of my life and that what I had learned would contribute immensely to my success as a trader for the remainder of my life as a stock trader. Everything I needed to know was going to be at my fingertips. I just had to remind myself every once in a while by reading my own material over and over again.

Joe had sent me a case of expensive champagne a few weeks after Taser crashed. A note attached to it said that he had been very happy with my work and that he would recommend me to his peers.

A week later while on vacation, I was sitting on the beach with my wife and my five-year-old girl. The waves on the ocean were gentle. The trade winds were blowing softly. It was nice and warm. I closed my eyes and settled down next to my wife as my daughter started her patient and persistent work on a brand-new sand castle. And I thought to myself that this is the good life. And I recalled that earlier that morning when I checked for the market news on the internet, there were over a dozen new IPOs lined up to come into the market within the subsequent two weeks.

The cycle was going to start once again. The new game was going to begin just as one game ended. The set up, the shake out, the fake out, the move, the end and the aftermath would all be the same. Only the players would most likely be different. And the pace of the game would more likely than not be different.

Somewhere among these new games being played out, there will occasionally be some money making opportunities yet again for the patient players like Boyd Hunt and Roger Stonybrooke. And they would wait and wait and bide their time until the game was just right. And when the time came, they would set up their plays the way only they knew how. There would be little doubt of the outcome for them. After all, they only placed their lines when odds were truly in their favor. And the best traders would continue to practice their craft in silence and in complete anonymity. They would come late to the party having ensured that indeed the party would be a success. Then they would leave the party early having had a good time. They would leave early enough to avoid the brawls that would come toward the end of a long party.

On my return from my vacation as I was sharing a drink with my wife after a good round of golf at the Biltmore in Phoenix, I saw a strange sight. I could not believe it at first. I saw Joe and Steve Sachs on the first tee ready to start a round of golf. It then dawned on me. I had been used by Joe. He and Steve Sachs had been the true big insiders of Taser. Steve Sachs had relied on Joe's venture capital money to set up the entire Taser move. Joe had called on me to get a feel and confirm his instinct that the stock was approaching a top. My report confirmed to him that the top was nearing. That was Joe's angle which had escaped me weeks earlier. I ordered a scotch to control my anger. A few sips later it seemed to have worked. Emotions were a sign of weakness. I had learned that from my two decades worth of dealing with the markets. And I also realized that Joe would have just gone on to use someone else if it had not been me. And he would have accomplished his goal whether or not I was involved. I was just another spoke on the wheel. I was replaceable.

Though things may seem to change, they remain the same. Human emotions and the markets have a connection that makes it impossible for one to function without the other.

For me at least until a stock that could be perfect shows up - cash would be king. And the market would continue to be right, as always.

ABOUT THE AUTHOR:

Brad Koteshwar is a lifelong student of the stock market. He started off working as a commodities broker. After some years, having been burned out by the stress of the high volatility and risk involved in trading commodities, he turned to the stock market. After years of learning by practice, Brad and his wife, Sheila, started an online newsletter (breakout123.com) in 2001 - right smack in the middle of a severe bear market. They subscribe to the philosophy, which is constantly imparted to their readers, that one has to be conservative and wait for the right stocks to show up before making any serious commitments. Brad ended up calling the top on Taser, the stock around which the story is written in this book, to the exact day in his newsletter.

www.ingramcontent.com/pod-product-compliance
Ingram Content Group UK Ltd.
Pitfield, Milton Keynes, MK11 3LW, UK
UKHW040015200726
13854UKWH00001B/206

9 781418 486884